WHAT'S WRONG WITH
DAY CARE

WHAT'S WRONG WITH DAY CARE

Freeing Parents to Raise Their Own Children

Charles Siegel

WITH A FOREWORD BY Christopher Lasch

Teachers College, Columbia University
New York and London

Published by Teachers College Press, 1234 Amsterdam Avenue, New York, NY 10027

Library of Congress Cataloging-in-Publication Data

Siegel, Charles.
    What's wrong with day care : freeing parents to raise their own children / Charles Siegel.
       p.   cm.
    Includes bibliographical references (p.   ) and index.
    ISBN 0-8077-3982-0 (cloth : alk. paper) — ISBN 0-8077-3981-2 (pbk. : alk. paper)
    1. Child care—United States.   2. Family policy—United States.   3. Work and family—United States.   I. Title.
    HQ778.63 .S54   2000
    362.82'0973—dc21   00-055205

ISBN 0-8077-3981-2 (paper)
ISBN 0-8077-3982-0 (cloth)

Printed on acid-free paper
Manufactured in the United States of America

08   07   06   05   04   03   02   01   8   7   6   5   4   3   2   1

[I]f the private sector is enlightened enough to provide slots for employees to park their cars, it can provide slots for employees' children [in day-care centers].

—Senator Barbara Mikulski (Dem., Md.)

CONTENTS

FOREWORD

In the debate about family policy, liberals claim to stand for the principle of "choice," but the policies they favor have the effect of forcing women into the workplace. If liberals were serious about freedom of choice, they might be expected to respect couples who choose to raise their own children instead of turning them over to professional caretakers. But the right of free choice, as liberals understand it, does not extend to "traditional" family patterns. People are free to choose, it seems, only if they choose to let economic pressures dictate their domestic arrangements.

Liberals demand a greatly expanded program of day care, supported by public funds, on the grounds that working women should not have to sacrifice their job prospects to the demands of full-time child care. In order to make it possible for women to compete with men in the job market, liberals argue, women have to be relieved of a burden men are not required to share. It is hard to argue with this reasoning as long as we ignore the predicament of women who enter the job market involuntarily. Many of those women would prefer to stay home with their children if they could find a way to make ends meet. Fairness requires a family policy that recognizes the validity of that choice and provides a child-care allowance (among other things) that would enable people to exercise it. The policies favored by liberals, however, discriminate against people who prefer "traditional" arrangements. The only choice liberals are prepared to recognize, notwithstanding their enthusiasm for the new "pluralism" of family types, is the choice in favor of the two-career family. Thus, Michael Dukakis, in his presidential campaign of 1988, recommended more than $2 billion for a federally funded system of day-care centers and nothing for people who keep their preschool children at home.

Since the kind of family policy favored by liberals is blatantly discriminatory, we might imagine that it rests on careful study of the psychological advantages of professional child care. We might be willing to accept discrimination if we could be persuaded that professional caretakers do a better job of raising children than their parents do. Most of the evidence, however, points to the opposite conclusion, as Charles Siegel shows in this admirably clear-headed analysis of family issues. The expansion of professional authority at the expense of the family has been justified on the grounds that the best way to "help" the family is to relieve it of its responsibilities. But the effect of this kind of help has been to weaken the ties between the generations, to reduce the emotional intensity of the parent–child connection, to deprive children of direct access to adult experience, and to produce a generation of young people who are morally and emotionally at sea, lacking any sense of participation in their culture's traditions or in its ongoing development.

Evidence concerning the effects of day care on character is inconclusive at best; yet our society has embraced day care, at least in principle, as the best way to provide for the needs of preschool children (or at least of their parents). In effect, Siegel argues, we have decided to experiment on a whole generation of young people not because we have much reason to believe that the experiment will succeed but because economic pressures dictate such a solution. Here is the heart of Siegel's case: the relentless expansion of our corporate-dominated productive system at the expense of everything else. Instead of building our economy around the needs of families, we have allowed economic imperatives to govern the structure of the family, the school, and every other agency of cultural transmission. No doubt, this is one reason everyone feels so harried today: "Our wealth," as Siegel points out, "makes us feel more impoverished than ever." More than any other single issue, the day-care question enables us to understand why "we feel harder pressed economically that people did in the past, even though we are much wealthier than they were."

Liberals ought to be deeply troubled by Siegel's book. They pride themselves on their "compassion," their commitment to "human rights," and their resistance to corporate domination; but if Siegel is right, they are playing the corporations' game when they acquiesce in the expansion of professional authority over the family. Their propaganda in favor of day care accords very well with the interests of corporations, many of which have discovered that "you can lower absentee rates and raise productivity levels through provision of quality child care." But conservatives should find Siegel's argument equally disconcerting. They talk about the importance of "family values" but are unwilling to restructure the workplace to make it possible for parents to raise their own children. "Any serious attempt to strengthen the family poses a more serious challenge to the modern economy than conservatives realize," Siegel writes, "and forces us to look far beyond what are usually thought of as child-care issues." If conservatives mean what they say about the superiority of parental child care, they will have to admit the need for family allowances and flexible work schedules. But this is only the beginning, according to Siegel. They will also have to recognize how deeply the family problem is embedded not only in the structure of the workplace but in the design of cities, the cult of economic growth, and a wasteful and ecologically unsound conception of the good life. The physical separation of the home and the workplace, suburban sprawl, the erosion of neighborhoods, the collapse of public transportation, and the domination of urban geography by the needs of the corporate economy have all contributed to the weakening of the family. A strong family requires an efficient system of public transportation, decentralized production, strict controls on real estate development, and a less wasteful standard of living—none of which conservatives are willing to countenance.

The great value of Siegel's book is that it shows how family issues cut across conventional debates between the left and the right. Neither liberals nor conservatives appreciate the complexity of these issues or the sweeping nature of the solutions required. Liberals have put forward a panacea—universal, federally funded day care—that merely compounds the problem that it claims to solve, while conservatives have contented themselves, for the most part, with moralizing about motherhood. Both parties in the day-care debate are too heavily committed to the existing economic system and to the principle of unlimited economic growth to criticize its by-products effectively. If we mean what we say when we claim to be a child-centered society, we are going to have to reject prefabricated political ideologies and think much more boldly than we have been accustomed to thinking about a wide range of issues.

Siegel shows why family issues are the best place to begin. I hope his book falls into the hands of readers who will approach it with an open mind. I hope it embarrasses those whose minds have hitherto remained closed. I hope, finally, that he is prepared for the abuse he will receive from those whose minds no argument can open. In some quarters, he is sure to be denounced as a benighted traditionalist, a defender of "patriarchy," a re-

actionary whose real intent is to re-enslave women—which will only prove
that his arrows have found their mark.

Christopher Lasch

*The author sent the first draft of this book to the late Christopher Lasch. Though
he did not know the author, Lasch liked the book and agreed to write a foreword
for it. After his death, this foreword was found, along with his correspondence with
the author, in the archive of Lasch's personal papers at the library of the University of Rochester.*

PREFACE

I have written this book because I think it is heartbreakingly sad that most American parents cannot cut back on their work for even a few years to take care of their own children. But I have also written this book because I think child-care issues raise larger questions about the American economy and about conventional social policy.

This book keeps returning to a central paradox of the modern economy. A century ago, 95 percent of all American women were able to care for their own preschool children at home: The only people who could not do this were the poorest of the poor. Today, the average family earns more than six times as much as it did a century ago, but most families feel they cannot afford to take time off from work to stay at home with their own children. We can reject the rigidly defined sex roles of a century ago but still ask why the modern economy has failed families in this way.

To let more families care for their own preschool children, we need to reform our child-care policies. Currently, federal and state tax laws and most private programs give funding to all parents who put their children in day care and give nothing to parents who cut back on their work hours to care for their own children. For example, most of the funding from the federal child-care tax credit goes to affluent dual-income families, only 3 percent goes to families with incomes below the 30th percentile, and none at all goes to families who care for their own children at home. We need more funding for child care, but we also need fair funding for child care—funding for families who need help paying for day care and also for families who need help to stay at home with their own children. Just as important, we need flexible work hours, so men and women who are new parents have the option of working part time without losing their jobs.

But to let more families care for their own children, we also need broader changes in our economy. Today, even if we offered flexible hours, most people would not be able to take advantage of them, because they have to work full time just to get by. The unbridled growth economy promotes—and in many ways, requires—a vicious circle of overspending and overworking that does not leave us enough time for our children. Growth threatens our families and communities, just as surely as it threatens the global environment. The central challenge of the twenty-first century is to shift to an economy that is sustainable both ecologically and socially.

But when it comes to child care, many policy makers do not see this problem at all. They just demand more funding for day care: The latest idea is to promote the development of children's brains by putting them in high-quality day care beginning at the age of 4 or 5 months. On environmental issues, social policy makers have new ideas, but on child care and on many other social issues, many are still stuck with the old progressive ideology of a century ago.

At the beginning of the twentieth century, social reformers had unlimited faith in science, technology, and economic growth. They believed in a utopia where people would work in factories and industrial farms designed by engineers; live in cities of steel, concrete, and glass designed by urban planners; and put their preschool children in programs designed by educators and developmental psychologists. These reformers have lost much of their influence, because a century of experience has punctured this ideal: It doesn't work, and if it did, it would look more like an air-conditioned nightmare than like utopia.

We need a new political direction that insists on modernizing selectively—using the technological economy when it actually is useful and limiting the technological economy when it threatens to overwhelm our environment, our neighborhoods, and our families.

I think child care is a key to this new direction. Our children are so obviously important that child care is the one issue that will let people see through the growth economy.

People are becoming dissatisfied. According to a recent survey, 70 percent of men in their 20s and 30s would give up some pay for more time with their families. Young men are actually more willing to give up pay for family time than young women, a dramatic change from earlier generations. It seems that both men and women are looking for more balanced lives.[1]

When people begin to ask themselves why Americans a century ago could care for their own preschool children while today's far more affluent Americans cannot afford to, we will begin the shift from manic growth to an economy that is more sustainable and far more satisfying.

1

THE FAMILY IN PERSPECTIVE

THE TRADITIONAL FAMILY

We often hear that most Americans no longer live in traditional families, with fathers who go to work and mothers who stay home with the children. But this "Ozzie and Harriet" style family is *not* the traditional family: It is the early form of the modern family, which is now changing into the late modern family. In the nineteenth century, as the Industrial Revolution began, it became common for one parent to leave home and go to work in a factory or an office. Now, both parents leave home to go to work.

In the early nineteenth century, most Americans lived on family farms. Even people who lived in towns often worked at home in family businesses. Both the husband and the wife stayed home, and both the husband and the wife worked. Of course, this was a sexist society, and work was assigned on the basis of gender. The husband plowed the field, chopped the firewood, and built fences; and the wife stayed around the house to take care of the children, can vegetables, and do the laundry. Men were in charge of family life and public life: They owned and controlled their families' property, and women were not allowed to vote. Despite the inequalities, though, and despite the long, wearying hours of work, many of us living today— at a time when most Americans work for corporations, live in housing tracts, and eat at McDonald's—cannot help but admire the independence of the traditional American family that worked its own land, built its own home, and grew its own food.

What we now call the "traditional family," with a wife who stays at home and a husband who goes to a factory or office to work, first became common in American cities in the 1830s and 1840s. Because of the Industrial Revolution, men began to earn their livings as hands in factories or as clerks in offices and women became homemakers. This sort of family—with an absentee father who spent 72 hours a week at the mill—was a direct result of economic modernization, and it is a mistake to call it the traditional family. It is the early form of the modern family, which appeared because many economic activities were being taken over by the market economy but home production remained important enough and time consuming enough that full-time housewives were still needed.

During the nineteenth century, the woman's role began to lose the dignity that it had in traditional economies, because production in the money economy was considered more important than production for use. The late nineteenth century in America—the Gilded Age—was a time when the country dedicated itself to accumulating money and power for their own sake. In 1800, women who worked at home were considered productive workers, like men who worked at home, but by 1900 the census listed them as dependents, along with infants, the sick, and the elderly.[2]

The upper and middle classes idealized the woman's role. She was considered a sort of ministering angel who created a home filled with comfort and humanity, so her husband and children could come home to a place better than the cold, competitive outside world. But this notion that women were too good for the cruel world of business was obviously condescending. Upper-class husbands spent their time downtown at Wall Street piling up profits; their wives spent their time uptown at the fashionable shops spending those profits; and everyone knew who was really more powerful and more important.

The working- class majority could not afford uptown shopping or servants. Wives had to work hard cooking, and cleaning, and canning, and mending, and doing the laundry, and caring for the children; and their husbands had to perform repetitive factory work for 12 hours a day to earn subsistence wages. Despite all their work, people looked down on the housewife's job: They were considered dependents, supported by their husbands, and their long hours of hard work were becoming invisible. Americans no longer had much use for the old Jeffersonian ideal of self-reliance: They considered the money economy all-important, and they were losing sight of the home economy.

During the twentieth century, the typical housewife's life became more comfortable and emptier. More and more things that used to be made at home were bought instead. As mass production cheapened consumer goods, people started buying their clothes off the rack instead of making

their own and buying Campbell's soup instead of canning their own vegetables. Labor-saving appliances, such as washers and dryers and dish-
washers, let the housewife do her remaining chores more quickly.

There were some attempts to dignify the housewife's remaining duties
by saying they were a science that required special training—the schools
started teaching girls what they called "home economics"—but the hand-
writing was on the wall. With fewer chores to do at home and with children starting school at an earlier age, women began going out into the world
of business. In the nineteenth century, for example, secretaries were always
men; but early in the twentieth century, women took over this job.

Today, the market economy is taking over last bits of work that people
still do for themselves. A few decades ago, for example, families cooked
almost all their meals, but the latest estimate is that 62 percent of meals
eaten inside American homes are fast-food or take-out:[3] People are too busy
to cook for themselves, and it is easier to pick up the family's dinner at
McDonald's while you are driving home from work. Most American families also have other people care for their preschool children, because they
are too busy to stay home with the children themselves. It is most convenient to pick up your children at the day-care center after picking up your
dinner at McDonald's, to avoid the trouble of taking them in and out of
the car seat an extra time.

Until recently, child care was the last productive activity of the family
that was still considered essential. As women entered the work force en
masse during the 1960s and 1970s, though, our society devalued the work
of caring for children at home, just as it had devalued other forms of home
production in the past. Preschools and Head Start programs could do a
better job of raising children than the family, because they were designed
by developmental psychologists. Old-line liberals like Hillary Clinton and
Rob Reiner still believe this, but their faith was much more common during the 1960s and 1970s. Once we no longer took the family's work seriously, divorce and illegitimacy increased dramatically: During the 1960s
and 1970s, social scientists argued that children were resilient and recovered quickly from divorce and that single mothers could raise children as
well as couples by putting their babies into day-care centers. People believed all this with little or no evidence, because they took it for granted
that the modern economy could do anything better than the home economy.

BLIND PROGRESS

As women entered the work force, there was a push to do *something* about
child care. Because everyone assumed it was inevitable that the money

economy would continue to displace the home economy, we adopted child-care policies that make people even more dependent and more powerless to do for themselves, such as the federal child-care tax credit. Because these policies are designed to fit families into the money economy, they help families who need child-care services and ignore families who care for their own children at home.

If modernization reaches its logical conclusion, every productive activity that people used to do for themselves will be replaced by goods and services that the modern economy provides for them. We do not realize how far the change has gone already. Most American cities, for example, are now built in a way that makes it impossible to get around by walking, the main form of transportation in American cities until the middle of the twentieth century. Instead of walking, modern Americans have to consume transportation—cars and gasoline provided by the corporate economy or mass-transit provided by the state. And instead of watching their children, they consume day care.

Policy makers tend to take a "pragmatic" approach to these issues. Rather than thinking critically about whether our economy is heading in the right direction, they gather statistics on current trends, which show that demand for child care or transportation is increasing and that supply is not keeping up. Then they translate the gap between supply and demand into an assessment of future "needs."

This sort of technocratic planning is profoundly wedded to the status quo. It makes it impossible to think politically about the trends that are being studied—to decide if they are trends that we should support or trends that we should try to change.

This sort of planning was used to build our urban freeway systems during the 1950s and 1960s. Automobile traffic was becoming more and more congested every year; traffic engineers gathered the statistics, projected future traffic volumes, and used this "objective" methodology to determine the needs for new roads; and the federal government funded new freeway systems to accommodate these "needs." Yet it was clear by the end of the 1960s that the highway engineers' attempts to solve traffic problems had actually made these problems worse: Building freeways to accommodate projected traffic encouraged people to drive more, and freeways that the engineers had predicted would accommodate traffic for decades were overcrowded a few years after they were completed.[4] In retrospect, most city planners agree that we would be far better off if the funding for our urban freeway systems had been spent in a more balanced way, with much of it going to public transit in older, pedestrian-scale neighborhoods. But technocratic planners, who project existing trends to determine future "needs," could not even consider that possibility.

Liberal proposals on child-care policy are based on this same sort of planning. They produce statistical studies to prove that the supply of child-care centers is not keeping up with the demand, and they conclude that the government should spend billions of dollars on child care to keep up with these projected "needs." This is called blind progress.

They do not mention statistics that challenge these trends. For example, we often hear that both parents now work in most families with preschool children, but we rarely hear about the surveys that show that 65 to 80 percent of all families with preschool children would rather care for own children at home if it were economically possible.[5]

Because we believe we need more day care, the federal tax laws allow a tax credit for child-care expenses of up to $960[6] and allow employers to provide up to $5,000 of tax-free child-care benefits. Under this law, a young dual-income couple—let's imagine that she is a lawyer and he is an accountant—who earn $110,000 per year and have two preschool children are entitled to a federal tax credit of $960 to help them pay for child care. If one of their employers provides a child-care plan, because the tax law encourages it, they could also get a tax-free subsidy of up to $5,000 per year.

On the other hand, imagine that this couple believes it is more important to raise their own children than to earn extra money. Let's say that they were both lucky enough to get part-time jobs in their own fields, each working 20 hours a week at their regular pay, rather than being forced to take the sort of low-paying jobs that are usually available to people who work part time. If they were to sacrifice $55,000 per year of income in order to do what they believe is a better job of raising their children, under the current tax laws they would get no government tax subsidy and no subsidy from their employers.

We are doing much the same thing with child care now that we did with freeways a few decades ago. We dealt with traffic problems by subsidizing freeways, but we found that people drove more and that congestion kept getting worse. Now we are dealing with child-care problems by subsidizing day care, and we find that more parents of preschool children work full time and join the crowd of parents looking for day care.

Though conservatives have blocked massive government spending on day care, corporations are becoming more responsive to their employees' "need" for child care. They find that providing day care has a real economic benefit, because it reduces employee turnover. Child-care advocates say that on-site day care "binds" workers to their employers.

Everyone pays for these subsidies, directly or indirectly. When the government subsidizes day care, you pay for it in higher taxes, whether you use it or not. When corporations subsidize day care, the cost is passed on in the form of higher prices and lower wages for all employees, whether they use the day care or not. As a result, people who compare the costs of raising their children themselves with the costs of putting them in day care are more likely to decide that they cannot afford to take care of their own children, however much they want to.

People who take care of their own children could become rare in some parts of the country during the next few decades—just as people who walk became rare in many American neighborhoods during the 1950s and 1960s, as cities were rebuilt around freeways.

THE LIMITS OF GROWTH

Child-care advocates claim that, whether you think it is good or bad, it is inevitable that more children are going to be in day care as more women work—and since children are going to be in day-care centers anyway, we should spend the extra money to make sure they are in high-quality day-care centers. Their policies would put people who care for their own children at even more of an economic disadvantage, but history seems to come uncomfortably close to confirming their view. If the money economy has been growing and taking over the productive activities of the home since the Industrial Revolution began, isn't it inevitable that the trend will continue?

It did seem inevitable early in the twentieth century, when progressives and feminists developed the current approach to child care, at a time when everyone believed that you could not stop modernization and progress. But during the past few decades, we have begun to see that there are limits to economic growth: Growth is useful up to a point, but it can destroy the natural and social systems that it is based on if it is carried beyond that point.

The ecological limits of growth are widely understood. We are all familiar with the greenhouse effect, ozone depletion, and acid rain. There have been international efforts to deal with these problems, with some success, but it will be much more difficult to deal with them as the world economy continues to grow during the twenty-first century.

There is a direct connection between economic growth and changes in the family. To put it in the simplest and starkest form, a society where both men and women work full time outside the home needs twice as large a money economy as a society where only men work full time outside the home. With twice as large a work force, you need to produce roughly twice as much to avoid unemployment. It is ecologically destructive to back day-care policies that promote faster economic growth by encouraging everyone to work full time: The challenge that we face as women enter the work force is to find new ways of working that let both men and women share the paid work of the money economy and the unpaid work of the home economy.

Yet we have already gone far enough that even providing universal day care would not have a major effect on economic growth. Women have been moving into the work force all through this century, and now even women in "traditional" families usually just take off a few years from work when their children are young. Moving all our preschool children into day care and all our older children into extended after-school care would add to economic growth and the ecological crisis, but only marginally.[7]

Yet some social critics have argued that there are also social limits to growth. If the economy expands beyond a certain point, it can create overwhelming social and psychological costs. We may be reaching this point: People have been becoming more powerless and more dependent on the economy ever since the beginning of the Industrial Revolution, but only in the last few decades has modernization gone far enough to cause increased suicide, drug abuse, crime, and random violence.

Universal day care could push us beyond the social limits of growth. There have not been adequate empirical studies of the psychological effects of day care, but we will see that historical studies of child-rearing and character suggest that children who are in day care full time may suffer subtle psychological damage as adults. They may not have noticeable psychological symptoms. On the contrary, they may be very "well-adjusted" and they may consider themselves happy—but they do not seem to have thought very deeply about what it means to be happy. They lack inner life, lack any strong commitment to ideas or to other people, and lack autonomy. If they get a steady nine-to-five job right after graduating from school, they will be quite contented: Because of their lack of inner life, they work well in groups and are not likely to rock the boat. But if they somehow slip through the cracks and do not fit into the organized system, their lack of inner resources makes it likely that they will become alcoholics, drug abusers, criminals, or suicides.[7]

These ideas about the effects of day care are tentative, but it is clear that we should proceed slowly and cautiously with a sociopsychological change as profound as moving most young children out of their families and into day care. We should have the chance to observe adults who were in day-care centers and extended after-school care all through their childhood and to study the effects that it had on their character during their entire adult lives before committing all of our children to this sort of upbringing.

Instead, we are pushing a generation of children into day-care centers, with virtually no thought about its moral and psychological effects.

Articles in the press that begin by saying that more and more families must put their children in day care, and then go on to talk about what kinds of day-care centers are best, are like the articles written decades ago that began by saying energy consumption would inevitably double every 10 years and then went on to talk about whether it was best to build more nuclear power plants or strip-mine more coal. Unbridled economic growth can do as much damage to the social environment as it can do to the natural environment. When you project current trends, you have to consider whether they are sustainable before you say that they are inevitable.

THE 80-HOUR WEEK

It is time to ask fundamental questions about the modern economy, not only because its "inevitable" trends look more and more dangerous but also because it is failing to keep its promises.

From the early twentieth century through the 1960s, economists and the general public believed that prosperity would bring us both higher income and more leisure time. The length of the average workweek went down from 72 hours in the early nineteenth century to 40 hours by the 1930s. Increasing leisure time was another economic trend that everyone said was inevitable: economists explained that, as technology became more productive and hourly wages went up, workers could afford to buy more goods and services and could also afford to work fewer hours.

Popular magazines ran articles predicting that automation would be so advanced by the twenty-first century that people would need to work only a few hours a week to produce all the goods and services that they wanted. Some economists said that the government should spend billions of dollars on recreational programs to help people fill their leisure time. Pessimists said that, despite the government programs and the new gadgets they had, people would be bored to death with so little work to do.

Nobody looking at economic history a few decades ago would have said it was "inevitable" that parents in the twenty-first century would have to work such long hours that they would not even have enough free time to take care of their own children. If the economic trend toward a shorter workweek had continued, it would have made day-care centers unnecessary.

Economists and journalists were still predicting that leisure would increase during the 1950s and 1960s, but these predictions were already obsolete by that time. From the end of World War II through the 1960s, the workweek remained at 40 hours. The trend toward shorter work hours, which had seemed to be a basic fact of economic progress ever since workers' living standards had begun to rise in the nineteenth century, stopped completely during the most affluent postwar decades, when income grew more quickly than ever before.

Since then, work hours have actually increased overall, and most families find that both spouses must work. A few decades ago, the typical American family was supported by a man working 40 hours a week. Now, the typical family works an 80-hour week—and most families seem to think that they need two incomes just to pay for food, housing, and other necessities. As a result, Americans have less time for their children—10 hours per week less today than in 1970.[8]

The most remarkable fact about the modern economy is almost never mentioned. The economic statistics show that, after adjusting for inflation, the average American is more than twice as wealthy now as in 1960 and four times as wealthy as in 1920.[9] Yet Americans feel less affluent and more financially pressed now than they did in 1960. Back then, we felt that our material prosperity was a bit overwhelming, and books such as *The Affluent Society* and *The Waste Makers* were best-sellers;[10] but now that we are twice as wealthy, the average family feels it is just getting by.

In 1960 or in 1920, everyone felt sorry for families that were so poor that the wife could not afford to take off even a few years from work to take care of her own children before they started school. That was rare decades ago, but now that we are so much wealthier, it has become common.

You can begin to appreciate the paradox of the modern economy if you imagine what Americans living in 1920—when cars were first becoming available to the middle class rather than being luxuries for the rich—would think if we told them that most American families today can afford two cars but cannot afford to take the time off to raise their own children. They would think that something was wrong, morally wrong, with people who care more about a crazy extravagance like having two cars than they care about their own children.

And you can begin to appreciate the burden that the modern economy imposes on us if you consider what people who lived in American cities and towns in 1920—people who walked to Main Street to do their shopping and who commuted to work on trolley cars—would think if they heard that today's American family absolutely needs two cars, that most people who live in American cities cannot go out to buy a cup of coffee or a newspaper, cannot take their children to school, and cannot get to work without using a car.

Today, Americans do not want the rigid gender roles of the 1920s, which forced mother to stay at home and forced father out of the home; most of us would rather have both parents share the work of earning a living and share the work of raising children. Still, it should give us pause to consider what the people who lived back in 1920 would think about the way we live today—about how much we have to work and how much we have to spend just to get by. It should make us ask fundamental questions about the modern economy and wonder whether a simpler way of life would be more satisfying.   ·

A NEW FEMINISM

Modern feminists have focused on women's right to work in the money economy. Like other Americans, they have devalued the home economy.

At the turn of the twentieth century, feminists began to believe that economic progress would move all work out of the home and into the money economy, a common idea at the time, and they hoped this change would free women from their traditional roles. During the 1960s, Betty Friedan revived the feminist movement by complaining that women were stuck in their homes and ridiculing what she called "the happy housewife heroine."[11] The women's movement of the 1960s and 1970s encouraged women to move into the work force en masse—and to prove they were as good as men by devoting themselves to their jobs rather than to their families.

This is a failure of modernism, not of feminism itself. Everyone should be able to see the obvious rightness of feminism's central principle: The feminist movement made people aware that women are fully human and should not be second-class citizens. When it began, most women did not have their own identities. Women not only took their husband's names; they were expected to live for the sake of their homes, husbands, and children, and only men were expected to have lives of their own.

Today, we need a new feminism that supports equality for women without idolizing the modern economy. A few feminist writers have pointed in this new direction, criticizing our belief that the money economy is more important than the home and neighborhood economy—which really means that men's work is more important than women's traditional work. Their thinking could move us toward larger social and economic changes, which would restore the balance between the money and home economy and leave people with more time for themselves, their families, and their communities.

Conventional feminists have lost much of their influence, because they refuse to deal with the problems Americans have today. Many parents find it hard to fulfill their basic responsibilities to their children because of high rates of divorce and unwed motherhood. Even intact families find it hard to care for their own children, because most need two incomes to get by. Only about 15 percent of Americans still live in "traditional" families with fathers who work and mothers who stay at home. You are not saying any-thing about the problems of American families today if you are still criti-cizing Ozzie and Harriet.

Today, most Americans live in fully modernized families. Both par-ents work, and the children are in day care or school full time. Families are so entangled in the money economy that they do not have time for child care or other work in the home economy. It is time to stop criticizing the "traditional family" and to start focusing on the problems of the modern family.

2

MODERNIZING AWAY
THE FAMILY

FAMILIES TODAY

Child-care advocates use the statistics about the current state of the American family to prove that we need to spend more money on day care, but they usually lump together statistics about two very different trends. On one hand, women's entry into the work force will redefine the family, but it will not necessarily weaken the family. On the other hand, high levels of divorce and unwed motherhood do make families weaker and less able to care for their own children.

Changes in the role of women have happened extremely quickly. In 1960, less than 19 percent of married women with children under 6 years of age were in the work force; today 63.5 percent of married women with children under age 6 are in the work force.[12]

The entry of women into the work force is historically unprecedented, and it should make us rethink the relationship between work and family life. Most of the current talk about child-care policy underestimates its importance. Child-care advocates just ask for more money for day-care programs to help people fit into the economic system as it is now organized, instead of talking about the larger economic and social changes needed to balance work and family. We can accommodate these changes in women's roles and leave the family stronger than ever, if we muster the political will needed to make the economy work for families.

Yet the statistics also point to a real breakdown of the American family. The divorce rate soared during the 1960s and 1970s—the rate in 1980 was over 250 percent of the rate in 1960[13]—before stabilizing at an unprecedentedly high level. About half of all first marriages now end in divorce.[14]

The number of unwed mothers grew dramatically and did not level off until the late 1990s. In 1960, only 5 percent of children were born to unmarried mothers. Today, the figure has gone up to about one-third. In just a few decades, the number of children born to unmarried mothers increased from 1 in 20 to about 1 in 3, from a figure so small that it was negligible to a figure so large that it is historically unprecedented.

Today, 45 percent of children born to married couples will experience a divorce before they grow up,[15] and one-third of all children are born to unwed mothers, so about three-quarters of all American children will spend all or part of their childhood with a single parent.[16]

Increased divorce and unwed motherhood means that many families are less able to take care of their own children. Economic problems alone make life much harder for single parents. Just as important, taking care of children is a labor-intensive business, and single parents do not have enough time.

The American family is weaker than ever before, less able to do for itself. Child-care advocates are right to say that families need help, but the question is whether the policies they propose will strengthen the family or weaken it even further. We need to look more deeply at the historical roots of our problems and think about solutions that go further than just spending more money on day-care centers.

People seem to think that the crisis of the American family began in the 1960s or 1970s, but in reality the American family has gone through a series of crises since modernization began taking parents out of the home. There was widespread concern about a crisis of "paternal neglect" caused by industrialization in the 1830s. There was equally widespread concern about the "New Woman" at the turn of the twentieth century, which led to the familiar progressive approach to helping the family by having expert professionals relieve it of its burdens. Looking at it in historical perspective, we can see that modernization weakened the family as the formal economy took over most of its functions and that the progressives' policies made the family even weaker by taking away its most important remaining function, raising children.

THE FIRST FAMILY CRISIS

"Paternal neglect" was "epidemic,"[17] according to an article in *Parents Magazine,* and magazines were filled with similar stories for two decades, as Americans worried that a crisis of paternal neglect was transforming the family.

The decades were not the 1960s and 1970s: This article appeared in 1842, and magazines were filled with talk about the crisis of paternal neglect during the 1830s and 1840s, as the American family changed dramatically because men began to leave their family farms and businesses to work in factories and offices, so they no longer had time to raise their children.

Early American families were rigidly controlled by fathers. Women were considered to be weaker than men, more subject to temptation ever since Eve ate the apple, and their husbands had the responsibility of watching over them. Fathers also had the primary responsibility for raising and disciplining their children. This view of the father's role was most pronounced among the Puritans, who believed that people were born sinful and needed strict discipline, but it was also held generally. Failures in childraising were blamed on the father's failure to discipline children properly. In the rare cases where they were divorces, American courts invariably gave fathers custody of the children so that they could continue to raise them. Common law held that children, like all the other assets of the household, were the father's property.

Things began to change when the Industrial Revolution came to American cities in the 1830s and 1840s. Men who worked in the new economy were rarely home—office or factory jobs typically took 12 hours a day, 6 days a week—so mothers had to take over the work of running the household and raising the children.

Early feminists, such as Catharine Beecher, tried to give women more power by emphasizing that men and women had "separate spheres": Men should run the workplace, but women should run the home. Beecher made this point in her first book, *The Elements of Mental and Moral Philosophy, Founded Upon Experience, Reason, and the Bible,* published in 1831, in which she argued that women were morally superior to men because of their greater capacity for self-sacrifice—introducing the gender stereotypes that became common during the Victorian period. She made the same point more strongly in *The American Woman's Home Companion,* published in 1869, an immensely popular work that she co-authored with her sister, Harriet Beecher Stowe.[18]

After the Civil War, when industrialization had gone far enough that the majority of Americans no longer lived on family farms, the idea that mothers were responsible for raising children became so ingrained that courts generally gave mothers custody of children after a divorce: What was called the "tender years doctrine" held that young children need a mother's nurturing. Likewise, if child-raising failed, it was blamed on problems caused by a failure of maternal nurturing.[19] By the late nineteenth century, books on child-raising were addressed exclusively to mothers, ignoring the father's role completely.

The Industrial Revolution created the Victorian ideal of the family. There was a cult of domesticity: Home was the place where you could find the human warmth that was lacking in the impersonal, competitive market economy, a "haven in a heartless world." Rather than being the weaker vessel, more subject to temptation, women were considered purer than men: Men's behavior in the economy was motivated by self-interest, while women's behavior at home was unselfish and motivated by higher ideals. In a reversal of the Puritans' view that the father was the religious leader of the family, women took responsibility not only for raising their children but also for introducing their husbands to the higher things in life. This was a running joke in the old comic strip "Bringing Up Father" (which first appeared in 1913), where Maggie was always trying to force fine music and refined conversation on her husband Jiggs, and he was always trying to sneak out of the house to spend his time smoking, drinking, and playing cards.

Though it compromised with modernization and let the industrial economy weaken the father's role, the Victorian family still worked. For example, crime and births to unwed mothers both declined by almost half during the Victorian period[20]—a remarkable achievement at a time when rapid urbanization was unmooring people from the communities that had traditionally controlled their behavior. Perhaps it was because the market economy seemed so cold and ruthless that there was a stronger focus than ever on how important it was for the home to shelter children from the outside world and its bad influences.

THE TWENTIETH CENTURY VERSUS THE FAMILY

The crisis of the family intensified at the turn of the twentieth century, as modernization continued and began to weaken the mother's role as well as the father's. In Victorian times, when industrialization had just begun, plenty of work was still left to the home. Today we can barely remember how much work it was just to do the laundry when you had to scrub each piece with a washboard in one tub, boil it on the stove in another tub, wring it out by hand, rinse it, hang it out to dry, and after it had dried, press it with a flat iron heated on the stove: Monday was washday, and it was called "blue Monday" because of this drudgery.[21] Likewise, sewing, mending, cooking, baking, cleaning, and raising children were hard, essential work. The home also provided most of its own entertainment; for example, middle-class families read novels aloud and played the piano. Finally, the home and voluntary organizations that relied on women's labor also had the responsibility for running charities that helped the poor.

During the twentieth century, the family lost most of these functions. The garment industry that developed in New York early in the century provided cheap ready-to-wear clothes, making it unnecessary to sew your own. Mass-produced bread was so inexpensive that it became unnecessary to bake your own. Radio, movies, and television—what we now call the entertainment industry—made it unnecessary for families to read aloud or play their own music. The welfare state took over most of the charity work from volunteer groups. Kindergartens, nursery schools, and day-care centers took over much of the work of raising young children.

Before the turn of the twentieth century, progressives already believed that modernization would ultimately take over completely. In America, the most influential progressive was Edward Bellamy, whose 1888 novel *Looking Backward* described a man who fell asleep in 1887 and woke up in the year 2000, in a completely modern socialist society. The entire American economy was nationalized and managed by the government like an efficient factory. Every adult was required to be a member of the "industrial army" that mass-produced all the economy's standardized products. The industrial army also cooked all the food and served it in public dining rooms; the modern economy had taken over the work that used to be done at home.[22] Bellamy's novel was fantastically successful, and Bellamy Clubs or Nationalist Clubs (so called because they wanted to nationalize the economy) sprouted up all across America to spread its ideas.

Around the turn of the twentieth century, feminists also adopted the modernist faith: Charlotte Perkins Gilman was the most influential advocate of the idea that women would be liberated by modernization—after cooking, laundry, and child care were taken over by professionals. Victorian feminists had believed that women could elevate public life because of their focus on the home: One wrote that her goal was to "bring the home into the world . . . make the world home-like."[23] By contrast, Gilman was the first in a long line of modernist feminists who devalued the home and wanted to eliminate women's work completely: Women's work was mindless stuff that anyone could do, but men's work required skills and training.[24] (Could she have been thinking of factory work?)

Gilman began her career by working for Bellamy's Nationalist movement; she believed in gradual evolution of a socialist society and was sympathetic to the Fabian socialists but not to Marxists. Around the turn of the twentieth century, she started a movement to free women from housework by building feminist apartment houses, where people lived in kitchenless suites and the building provided collective eating, laundry, and child-care services. This was the direction of economic progress, Gilman said, "making a legitimate human business of housework; having it done by experts instead of by amateurs."[25] The housewife was a throwback to primitive times, badly in need of the benefits of industrial technology and the division of labor that went with it: "By what . . . miracle," Gilman asked, ". . . has the twentieth century preserved *alive* the prehistoric squaw!"[26]

During the first couple of decades of the twentieth century, the movement to build kitchenless houses, with collective cooking, child-care, and laundry services, became so influential that a major women's magazine wrote:

> The private kitchen must go the way of the spinning wheel, of which it is a contemporary.[27]

That quotation is not from a radical feminist manifesto of the 1960s. It was published in the *Ladies' Home Journal* in 1919—a sign of how influential modernism was at the time.

The Modern Family Crisis

Modernism moved quickly from the socialist fringe to the progressive mainstream. Around the turn of the twentieth century, progressive reformers declared that the American family was in crisis and gained widespread public support for their programs to help the family by relieving it of the burden of raising young children.

Reformers worried about the large number of children being produced by poor immigrant families, who were not equipped to raise them properly, and they also stirred up national concern about the well-being of families at the other end of the social scale.

One problem was what people at the time called the "New Woman." More and more women were going to college, joining organizations, and getting jobs—the proportion of married women who worked more than doubled between 1890 and 1910, from just under 5 percent to over 10 percent[28]—and many women seemed to prefer their work to having children. Theodore Roosevelt claimed that women's new "desire to be independent" was leading to "race suicide"[29] by lowering the birth rate among "the highest races."[30] But feminists argued that women were simply "following their work out of the home": Since the Industrial Revolution had stripped the family of most of its productive functions, it had become an emotional necessity for women to work so that their lives would not be empty.

Another problem was the sharply rising divorce rate. During the 1880s and 1890s, the number of divorces grew three times as quickly as the population, and Americans were shocked at the turn of the twentieth century to learn that we had the highest divorce rate in the world. Then the divorce rate doubled again between 1900 and 1920.[31]

Sociological explanations for these problems were readily available. For example, one sociologist wrote in 1915 that the traditional family was "unsatisfactorily adjusted to twentieth-century conditions" because the Industrial Revolution had taken away its functions and reduced it to "a temporary meeting place for board and lodging."[32] Likewise, in 1916, an article in the *American Journal of Sociology* explained that "the present instability of monogamous wedlock results from imperfect adaptation to modern society and industrial conditions."[33] The family was becoming obsolete as a result of modernization.

This was the beginning of the continuing crisis of the family, which experts in social welfare kept announcing all through the twentieth century.

The Therapeutic State

It was clear from the beginning what the modern approach to helping the family would be.

Early in the twentieth century, there was a dramatic increase in technological control over ordinary people's activities. Nineteenth-century factory workers still used many their older crafts skills and knowledge, for example, but the twentieth century saw the rise of "scientific management": Managers broke down the workers' tasks into their simplest parts and used time-motion studies to design the production process more efficiently. Workers performed simple repetitive tasks, because the scientific managers built all the skills into the design of the factory.

Obviously, the way to help the family was to extend the same sort of scientific control to people's private lives as well as to their work. Teachers, doctors, guidance counselors, psychologists, social workers, and other professional experts began to supervise or take over the task of raising children.

The therapeutic state was most active in the slums, where the need was greatest. Social work established itself as a profession during the early decades of the twentieth century, centered in the settlement houses at first but incorporated into the government before long. In addition, the juvenile courts were established in 1899, and under the doctrine of *parens patriae*, they treated children as wards of the state. Reformers congratulated themselves on giving up the old, retributive idea of justice and adopting this enlightened therapeutic approach. But the new approach proved to be a two-edged sword: Since the courts existed to help the accused, there was no need to protect the defendants' rights or to limit the amount of help given. The juvenile courts ignored elementary rights, such as trial by jury, representation by counsel, and public trial, until the Supreme Court restored some of these rights in the 1960s. And even if a crime would have been punished by a small fine in the ordinary courts, the juvenile courts could confine the criminal for decades if the cure took that long.[34]

Despite the therapeutic control involved, social workers and the juvenile courts probably did more good than harm overall, since poor families really needed help to cope with a new world. The therapeutic bias did much more damage when the experts tried to help the entire population care for their children, not just the poor. When progressives focused on family policy early in the twentieth century, they made parents feel increasingly incompetent.

Progressive reformers named the twentieth century "the century of the child"—the title of a book published in 1900 by the Swedish feminist and progressive educator Ellen Key. Theodore Roosevelt convened the first White House Conference on Children in 1909. The U.S. Children's Bureau was founded in 1912. There was a strong national movement to strengthen the schools, in order to fill the vacuum created by the decline of the family: Ellen Richards, one of the founders of the profession of social work, argued in 1910 that the school is "fast taking the place of the home . . . because the home does not fulfill its function."[35]

Faith in the new science of psychology also helped to transfer child-raising from parents to experts. G. Stanley Hall, known as the founder of child psychology in the United States, did the most to spread the faith in this new science to the public. Hall was the first to invite Freud to speak in the United States, and before long every moderately educated American had heard at least two things about Freudian psychology: first, that the study of early childhood was a difficult scientific subject that ordinary people could barely understand, and second, that early childhood was the critical period of psychological development, so any errors parents made during these years could give their children "complexes" that would make them neurotic for life. Needless to say, this popular impression of Freud's theories did not give parents great confidence in their ability to raise their own children. It made them more eager than ever to get help from scientists and doctors.

Infants in School

Parents began starting children in school at earlier ages, since they believed that even the youngest children could benefit from programs based on the new findings of developmental psychology. Traditionally, children did not start school until they were 7 years old, but the age went down steadily throughout the twentieth century.

In 1852, Massachusetts passed America's first compulsory education law, which required children between the ages of 8 and 14 to attend school for at least 12 weeks each year. The short term shows that schooling was considered just a small part of a child's education. Because children were required to be in school when they were 8, most started schooling at age 7 and stayed at home with their mothers until they reached this age.

The idea that children should begin school at age 7 has a long history. In ancient Greece, boys generally began their formal education at this age. During the Middle Ages, the first 7 years of life were called "infancy,"[36] and children were left exclusively in the care of women until they reached that age and began their formal education, which involved apprenticeship plus a bit of schooling. By the seventeenth century, it had became common to finish school first and then begin work; the age when schooling began varied a great deal, but 7 was most common. One early school inspector commented that "children cannot be sent to school before the age of seven or eight."[37]

The same rule applied in early America. A Quaker pamphlet on child-raising written in 1730, for example, pointed out that a key turning point in children's lives occurred at age 7, when they started school, and that they should be cared for by their parents until then: "From the breast, and the arms, to the seventh year of age . . . our parents . . . keep us out of harm's way, clothe us and keep us whole and clean, and take care that we learn no ill words or manners."[38]

This idea that children should stay at home until age 7 was still intact in the late nineteenth century, when the first compulsory schooling laws required children to be in school at age 8, but then the age for starting school began to drop.

Around the turn of the twentieth century, kindergartens became popular among Americans.[39] Parents also began to send children to first grade at an earlier age, and compulsory education laws were changed during the first half of the century to require schooling at age 7 rather than 8. Children began first grade at age 6, so they started kindergarten at age 5.

During the 1950s, progressive suburban parents began sending their children to nursery school at age 3 or 4, to prepare them for kindergarten. A decade later, the federal government funded the Head Start program so that poor children could also have the benefits of nursery school.

All through history until the "century of the child," schooling began at age 7. In the early twentieth century, schooling began with kindergarten at age 5. In the mid-twentieth century, schooling began with nursery school or Head Start at age 3 or 4. We were well on the way to today's America, where parents put their children in preschools at the age of a few months so that they can get back to their jobs.

POSTWAR AMERICA

Pop social criticism looks back on the 1950s as the high point of the "traditional" family, but it does not make sense that the family would break down in just a few decades after its golden age. In reality, the traditional roles of the 1950s family were already stretched to the breaking point because the modern economy had taken over the family's work, filling our suburbs with bored housewives who sat at home with nothing to do. The left of the 1960s and 1970s did not see this because it continued the modernist attack on the "traditional" family, and it did not think about the new problems the family would face when modernization went further and women entered the paid work force.

Togetherness

There *was* a real revival of the family during the 1950s. After World War II, marriage and birth rates soared, divorce rates fell, people moved to the new suburbs for the sake of their families, and women became more likely to stay home than they had been earlier in the century. In 1954, *McCall's* magazine first talked about the new ideal of family "togetherness," a word that was used in popular magazines for the rest of the decade to describe the revival of the family.

But the ideal of togetherness was based on feelings of powerlessness. People retreated to their families to escape the technological economy, which had begun to look more impersonal and threatening than ever during the Depression and World War II.

The family revival of the 1950s did not last because people retreated to the family for emotional support but no longer believed it had any practical function. The suburban home of the 1950s was purely a center of consumption, because the modern economy had taken over virtually all its productive work, and the schools, nursery schools, and child psychologists were taking over the work of raising children. The suburban houses were filled with bored housewives, who were stultified because they had nothing to do and who became the eager readers of Betty Friedan's *The Feminine Mystique* a few years later.

Talcott Parsons, the most eminent sociologist of the time, developed a theory of the family that sums up the 1950s. Parsons said that the nuclear family was a psychological necessity because it was the one place where intense feeling was still possible in a world that was increasingly impersonal and competitive. The family met a deep human need for love and loyalty, which the larger economy did not satisfy. The family was needed for emotional reasons, even though it had lost all its economic functions.

Parsons believed the family would become more effective as it lost its economic functions, because it would specialize in its emotional functions and specialization increases efficiency. Yet he added that the family was stressed by being the one source of emotional comfort in our society—and he knew how to deal with this stress:

> It is, one might suggest, the "American method," to attempt to solve problems in foci of strain by calling in scientifically expert aid. In industry, we take this for granted. In human relations, it is just coming to the fore. The immense vogue of psychiatry, of clinical psychology and such phenomena are, we suggest, an index of the importance of strain in the area of . . . family and marriage relations.[40]

Parsons's theory sums up the conventional view of the family during the 1950s: Family togetherness is an emotional necessity, but the family must depend on the corporate economy for its economic survival, on the schools and nursery schools to raise its children, and on the psychologists to fix it when it breaks down.

The trouble with the theory of togetherness was its timing. Parsons claimed the family would become stronger by losing its economic and educational functions and specializing in providing emotional support. But the radical left of the 1960s rejected the family entirely as an institution, and the feminists of the 1960s and 1970s complained that housewives were bored because they had nothing to do: Thus the privileged children who had grown up in the child-centered suburbs of the 1950s led the revolt against the family.

The theory of togetherness collapsed during the 1960s and 1970s, with those decades' unprecedented increase in divorce, out-of-wedlock birth, and family breakdown. History proved that this theory was wrong. The family did not become stronger when it stopped doing productive work—not only economic work but even most of the work of raising children. Instead, people begin to consider it dispensable.

1960s Radicals

The left of the 1960s and 1970s was adamantly antifamily. Modernization had already taken away all the family's functions, and the left considered itself radical because it wanted to hammer the last nail into the coffin.

Radicals criticized the family by using Marxist theories that were invented during the nineteenth century and Freudian theories that were invented at the turn of the twentieth century, and they ignored the dramatic changes in the family that occurred during the twentieth century. There had been the beginnings of a different ideological approach during the 1950s and early 1960s, when many books were written about the "organization man's" lack of individuality and desire to fit in with the peer group,[41] but the New Left went back to older ways of thinking.

1960s and 1970s radicals claimed that our "repressive patriarchal society" had its psychological roots in infancy, when children internalized the repressive father to form the superego. This may have been true in Freud's Vienna, but not in postwar America. American mothers had begun to take over child-raising during the 1830s, and postwar sociologists considered this such a commonplace that they invented the word "momism" to describe the main problem of the American family.[42] Many went even further. For example, the classic study of the 1950s suburbs, *Crestwood Heights*, said that in middle-class families, both parents had abandoned their authority in favor of decision making that was "'democratic'—based on relatively free discussion, action only with the will of the majority, persuasion rather than force."[43] The repressive patriarchal upbringing that Freud had described and radicals criticized was already obsolete.

One best-selling book of the time was *Open Marriage: A New Life Style for Couples*,[44] by a husband–wife team who wrote that trust is important, but sexual fidelity is stifling and should be scrapped in favor of sexually open relationships that promote personal growth. Two years later (almost as if there were a cause-and-effect relation) another best-selling book was *Creative Divorce*, which reassured people that, though it was painful, divorce could be a liberating adventure that promotes personal growth. As evidence of how common the new view of the family was, the blurb on the cover of the mass-market paperback edition of this book, which calls it "The most challenging reading since *Open Marriage*," is quoted from a review in the *Ladies' Home Journal*.[45]

The academic left argued, with no evidence at all, that single motherhood did not have any ill effects on children, that the problems of single mothers were entirely the result of poverty and racial discrimination.[46] For example, the left was outraged when the Moynihan Report came out in 1965 and said that the rising illegitimacy was a threat to the well being of African Americans. The left said that the "matriarchal family" was an adaptation to Black circumstances, that it was just as valid as the "nuclear family" was for Whites, and that anyone who disagreed was a racist. The accusations of racism were so fierce that (as William J. Wilson said) social scientists were afraid to study the Black family for over a decade for fear of being labeled racists.[47] Yet the left also demanded more spending on Head Start programs, day care, after-school programs, and other social programs to help these single-parent families—though it seems odd that families who are so very well adapted need all the extra help.

Likewise, in the 1960s and 1970s the left argued that children recovered quickly from divorce, and this became the conventional wisdom. Academics used flimsy evidence to support this theory—some studies were actually done by asking mothers whether they thought their divorce had hurt their children[48]—and everyone was shocked when Judith Wallerstein published the first in-depth study of divorce in the 1980s, which found that divorce causes deep emotional damage to children that continues throughout their childhood and often well into adulthood.[49]

These ideas had consequences. Unwed motherhood became acceptable and common. Progressives sometimes claim that this has happened because poor women cannot find husbands with decent jobs, but, in reality, unwed births have increased most sharply among college-educated women in managerial and professional positions,[50] with Murphy Brown as the famous fictitious model. Divorce became something you did for the sake of your own fulfillment: Statistics and surveys show that the presence of children stopped inhibiting divorce after 1973.[51] After interviewing representative Americans, one team of sociologists found that many took a "therapeutic attitude" toward marriage, which "denies all forms of obligation and commitment in relationships, replacing them only with the ideal of full, open, honest communication among self-actualized individuals."[52]

You can still hear echoes of the ideology of the 1960s and 1970s on the American left. The attack on patriarchy, the attack on the "traditional" Ozzie and Harriet family, and other criticisms of the family that were developed during the nineteenth and early twentieth century are still repeated by feminists and leftists who came of age during the 1960s and 1970s. At some universities, they are still the politically correct orthodoxy that no one dares to criticize. These old ideas still have enough force to prevent us from developing new ideas about the family.

THE DECLINE OF THE LEFT

During the 1960s and 1970s, radicals argued that single motherhood was an alternative lifestyle, as valid as any other and more liberating. It was easy to romanticize unwed mothers in 1960, when they had only 5 percent of all children, but it is much harder now that one-third of all children are born to unwed mothers and 45 percent of the remainder will live with a single parent at some point because of divorce. By the 1980s, there were entire communities where more than 90 percent of the households were headed by unwed mothers, and they were filled with crime, violence, and hopelessness.[53]

Social scientists have developed a body of solid research showing that unwed motherhood and divorce hurt children. The most extensive statistical analysis was done by Sara McLanahan and Gary Sandefur, who found that children of unwed or divorced parents are twice as likely to drop out of high school as children from intact families,[54] are 1.5 times as likely to be idle (out of school and out of work) as children from intact families,[55] and are almost twice as likely to become unwed mothers as children from intact families.[56]

They also found that, contrary to the old leftist ideology, these children's problems are not caused only by poverty. They *are* very poor— the poverty rate for families headed by single parents is 26.5 percent, compared with just 5.3 percent for families headed by two parents[57]—but the damage caused by poverty accounts for only about half their disadvantage compared with children from intact families.[58] And when divorced parents remarry, although they regain ground economically, their children are no better off than children of divorced parents who do not remarry.

McLanahan and Sandefur studied high school dropout rates, idleness, and unwed motherhood because they are strongly correlated with economic success, but other studies have found that children from broken families suffer from a wide range of social pathologies. For example, children of single or divorced parents are more liable to depression and eating disorders, are more likely to abuse alcohol and drugs, are more likely to become juvenile delinquents and adult criminals, and are more likely to be sexually abused than children from intact homes.[59] A statistical review of 50 major studies showed that 60 percent of rapists, 70 percent of long-term prisoners, and 72 percent of adolescent murderers come from fatherless homes,[60] and the relationship between family structure and crime is so strong that, if you control for differences in family structure, race and class have no correlation with crime.[61] Most ordinary people now believe the same thing as the social scientists: The Million-Man March on Washington showed that many African American men realize that the most important thing they can do to help their community is to be responsible fathers.

Things finally got so bad that people began to lose their faith in progress and to reject the left's therapeutic approach to "helping" the family. Instead, they started to demand that parents take more responsibility for their children. And astoundingly, although they both remain very high, the divorce rate peaked and leveled off during the 1980s and the proportion of births to unwed mothers finally leveled off after 1994.[62]

These "inevitable" trends, used to justify more therapeutic interven-
tion in the family for a century, leveled off when people began to see that
children really do need intact families. It is by no means certain that things
will get better, but it at least seems possible.

Family Values

Conservatives were the champions of "family values" during the 1980s and
1990s. So far, the winners in the battle over the family have been right-wing
groups such as the Promise Keepers, fundamentalist Christians who want
to restore the man's place as the head of the family, and conservative social
theorists such as George Gilder, who says that men will turn to violent crime
unless they have the opportunity to sublimate their aggression by domi-
nating their families.[63] These people not only want to revive the family;
they also want to restore the patriarchal family, with the man at its head.

Even within the Democratic party, the left has been displaced by neoliberals, such as Bill Clinton, who take a middle-of-the road position in the
culture wars over the family, who want more day care and services but
who also want to reduce divorce and unwed motherhood. Leftists and
feminists lost much of their influence because they kept attacking the family
as a hotbed of patriarchy and repression at a time when the real problem
is family breakdown.

Thirty years ago, the radicals' attack on the family sounded liberating, but now they sound as if they are out of touch with reality. Judith Stacey
is one of the few writers today who still has this viewpoint, claiming that
as they divorce and remarry, Americans are replacing the oppressive patriarchal family with "postmodern family arrangements" that are "diverse
and innovative."[64] But it is hard to understand her optimism when you look
at the actual stories of the two California women whose soap-opera-like
family lives she tracks. One woman went through a divorce and an on-and-
off second marriage that drove her to try therapy and antidepressant drugs;
one of her sons was a high school dropout who was so rebellious that she
considered putting him in foster care; her other son was a drug user; and
her daughter was a born-again Christian who lived with a group that seems
almost like a cult. The other woman had a violent marriage that almost
collapsed several times before her husband died; one of her sons died in
an auto crash while driving his new BMW at 120 miles per hour; her other
son was a drug addict and dealer who spent years in jail; one of her daughters attempted suicide after she found that her husband, a drug user and
alcoholic, was seeing another woman; another daughter was an unwed
mother, who married a man who was not her child's father and divorced
him after he began to beat her.

Stacey says that as these people's households form and dissolve, they are creating a "new family diversity"[65] to replace the oppressive, monolithic nuclear family. But her stories actually show us that that ongoing family breakdown causes extreme pain to everyone concerned. Feminists are not going to win over the public with this vision of the family. Compared with this sort of "diversity," the Promise Keepers and the Million-Man March look good.

Stacey says that she grew up during the 1950s watching "Ozzie and Harriet" and "Father Knows Best" and wondering why her own family was not as perfect as families on television, until she realized during the 1960s how oppressive the patriarchal family was.[66] It seems that she is still so busy fighting these old battles that she refuses to look at the new problems of families today. But she must have some idea that the new family diversity does not add up to a comforting vision of the future, since she titled her book *Brave New Families*.

Even the academic left is beginning to admit that the 1960s antifamily ideology has failed, and old-line radicals such as Judith Stacey and Stephanie Coontz[67] are in danger of being displaced as academic favorites by neoliberals such as Cornell West and Sylvia Ann Hewlett—who worry about the ill effects of single-parent families but who refuse to see that the modern technological economy has undermined the family, who want to support families by promoting suburban affluence, and who call the 1950s the "golden age of the American family."[68] Now that the old 1960s radicals are being eclipsed by neoliberals with such conventional ideas, there is no longer any important radical view of the family.

The End of the Therapeutic

Both the old radicals and the neoliberals are still proposing policies to deal with child care and the family that take the same approach progressives have all through the twentieth century: They are still calling for programs that help families by taking over their responsibilities, rather than programs that would help families do more for themselves. They want to provide more day care, provide more Head Start programs, provide more extended care before and after the regular school day. And they want to go further than ever before: It is now acceptable to put children a few months old in day-care centers, and our most progressive cities keep schools open from 6:30 in the morning until 6:30 at night so that parents can drop off their children at extended-care programs before they commute to work and pick them up after they get back.

The changes that have been going on since the beginning of the twentieth century are reaching their logical conclusion. Yet the feeling of technological optimism that buoyed progressives a century ago is now gone. Most people no longer believe that modernization and science are creating a brighter world for our children. Rather than claiming that progress will bring us a better future, progressives usually argue that massive federal spending on day care and extended after-school care is needed just to help families survive—to keep children off the streets, to take care of all the children of single parents, and to help all the families that need two incomes. The old vision is not as attractive as it was a century ago: The left still wants more funding for professionally run day-care centers, built to government standards, but this no longer sound as appealing as successful families and neighborhoods.[69]

There is one place where the old technological faith still survives: Progressives are now arguing that brain scientists have proven we can improve child-raising if we put children in high-quality day-care centers during the first 3 years of their lives. For example, Hillary Clinton writes:

> Significant headway has been made in the field of biology, where researchers have begun to grasp how the brain develops. . . . Dr. Frank Goodwin, former director of the National Institute of Mental Health, cites studies in which children who could be described as being "at risk" for developmental problems were exposed at an early age to a stimulating environment. . . . At the age of four months, half of the children were placed in a preschool with a very high ratio of adult staff to children. . . . Those in the experimental group averaged 17 points higher in IQ tests.[70]

The benefits of these programs are exaggerated. For example, although IQ initially increases by 17 points, the gain diminishes over time and is less than 5 points by the time the children reach high school—not enough to make a significant difference in school achievement.[71] Though children who were in day care have higher scores than the control group of poor, at-risk children who did not go to day care, they still have much lower scores than the national average. Yet constant repetition has convinced middle-class parents that their children's brains would also be hard-wired to make them more intelligent if they were in day care during the first 3 years of their lives.[72]

Hillary Clinton is also in favor of the Healthy Start program, which sends social workers to the hospital to visit parents of newborn children who are at risk and to decide whether it is necessary to continue visiting these families. Although this program is now voluntary, Mrs. Clinton says we might do well to make it compulsory.[73]

This future of being managed by therapeutic experts sounds chilling. Do we really want to put 4-month-old children in preschool programs designed by scientists who have done research on "how the brain develops"—with Ritalin prescriptions for infants who do not fit in? Do we really want trained social workers to pay compulsory visits to newborn babies to make sure their families will raise them properly? If so, we might as well let the technocrats take control a few months earlier: If we provide federal funding for genetic engineering at the time of conception, maybe we can produce children who are guaranteed to be well adjusted.

Experts in social welfare stick to the therapeutic approach, though their ideas range from the most extreme to the most obviously inadequate. For example, one professor of public health at UCLA found in his research that suicide and violence among Americans 15 to 24 years old has tripled over the past 30 years, and so he made the following policy recommendation:

> Additional in-depth health education is required in the schools, and not only about basic things like brushing your teeth, but also about the more serious areas, like violence. . . . You have to begin earlier, like the fourth, fifth, and sixth grade.[74]

Even if they are not experts, most people can see that suicide and violence among young people have not increased dramatically just because we failed to spend enough on health education classes. They can see that the decline of the family and the changing ways in which we have raised our children over the past decades have had a deep effect on our national character.

Americans are no longer willing to support the left's usual therapeutic programs, but they may be ready to see that real social and economic changes are needed to preserve the family.

CHAPTER

3

PSYCHOLOGICAL EFFECTS
OF DAY CARE

THE REPRODUCTION OF CHARACTER

To address the causes of these problems, we must look at the effect of our child-raising methods on social character. It is a truism among social-psychologists that every society has mechanisms for reproducing the character structure it needs and that the methods used to raise the youngest children are crucial. For example, Erik Erikson has shown how different methods of breast-feeding and toilet-training created the different types of character demanded by the economies of different groups of Native Americans—a fierce, aggressive character among those who hunt buffalo, and a patient, acquisitive character among those who fish for salmon.[75] But you do not have to be a Freudian like Erikson to believe that the way children are raised during their earliest years has a permanent effect on their characters. The idea is very conventional.

Our society, more than any in the past, must make a deliberate political decision about how our children are raised. We can fund day-care centers, or we can fund child care in ways that make it easier for parents to take care of their own children.

You would expect that we would base this choice on careful thought about the effects of day care on social character. Instead, we seem to be experimenting on an entire generation of children without thinking at all about the moral and political effects of day care. The empirical studies of the subject look at whether children who were in day care are well adjusted—with adjustment defined in narrow ways that are easy for psychologists to measure. We could easily reach the point where the overwhelming majority of our children are raised in day-care centers before we have any idea of its deeper effects on social character.

There is some very basic work that shows the direction we should take when we study adults who were in day care as small children. The Israeli kibbutz can be seen as an early test of something resembling our current patterns of child care, because the children there are raised in common nurseries from earliest infancy, and Bruno Bettelheim has written a well-known and important study of how this form of child care affects social character. There have also been many studies of the changes in the American character during this century, as the role of the family in raising children declined and children were put in schools at an earlier and earlier age: The characterological changes that they describe are strikingly similar to the changes caused by kibbutz child-raising methods.

These studies can help us to understand how the American character has changed during recent decades and to see what questions researchers should ask when they study the psychology of American adults who were in day care as infants.

CHILDREN OF THE KIBBUTZ

Bruno Bettelheim's studies of children who grew up on the Israeli kibbutz are particularly compelling, because Bettelheim was biased in favor of the kibbutz's methods when he began his work. Before going to a kibbutz to observe it firsthand, he criticized psychologists who claimed that raising children institutionally damages their mental health, saying they assumed "child rearing methods that are standard in our middle-class culture are therefore best in all cultures."[76] He hoped to find methods of raising children on the kibbutz that could be applied in programs for poor, culturally deprived American children.[77] Yet, after spending time studying the kibbutz, he found that its method of raising children has destructive effects on personality.

On the kibbutz, children are taken away from their parents when they are 4 days old to live in separate children's houses, where four to six infants are taken care of by one *metapelet* (nurse). For the first 6 months of life, infants do not leave the children's house; their fathers and mothers go there to visit them. After they are 6 months old, they also visit their parents' rooms for 2 hours a day. At age 1 or 2, children are moved to the toddlers' house, where a group of about six are cared for by a *metapelet*; and at 3½ or 4, children are moved to the kindergarten house, where a group of about 18 children are cared for by a *metapelet* and a teacher. Adults and children all eat meals in a common kibbutz dining hall.

Many of these kibbutz practices are remote from anything that occurs in America. Others—for example, the fact that toddlers spend most of their time in a group of children of the same age—are closer than we would like to admit. In fact, the way most American toddlers are raised today is as close to the kibbutz's methods as it is to the way American toddlers were raised a few decades ago. Although we will look at some differences later in this chapter, the features of kibbutz child-raising that Bettelheim says are the most important psychologically do apply to American children who are raised in day-care centers, at least to some extent.

The most important feature of kibbutz child-raising is the reduced intensity of children's relationships with their parents. "Much of the waking time spent by the middle-class infant watching his parents," Bettelheim says, "the kibbutz infant spends watching his roommates."[78] When Bettelheim wrote, the challenges and satisfactions of life for typical middle-class American infants centered around their parents and perhaps one or two other people. Generally, such children became very accustomed to the ways that these few people behaved, learning to recognize and respond to subtle details of other people's behavior.[79]

Children became even more sensitive to their parents' behavior in some older European cultures. In the Netherlands, for example, babies traditionally were kept in their cribs during the first months of life; they were usually left alone except when the mother came to pick them up and feed them. Bettelheim uses this extreme example to show how "the mother's devotion to her infant when she is with him, compared to the lack of stimulation during the rest of the day, incredibly heightens the time when the mother does come; how it lays the basis for the wish, later in life, to find fulfillment in the deep and concentrated relationship to one other person— in adolescence through the single great friendship, in maturity through the marital relationship."[80]

The kibbutz's method goes to the opposite extreme. Infants are never alone. They are always surrounded by other children and by the *metapelets*. Unlike middle-class children, kibbutz children must learn to ignore the people around them—or at least to ignore the finer nuances of other people's behavior—so that they can cope with the constant stimulation around them.[81]

This lack of emotional involvement with their parents as infants makes it difficult for the children of the kibbutz to develop intimacy with others as they grow up.[82] Traditionally, middle-class children developed intense friendships as adolescents and went on to have intense relationships with their spouses and their own children. By contrast, from childhood through adolescence through adulthood, people on the kibbutz are oriented more to the group than to other individuals. Most adults who have grown up on the kibbutz have a weak emotional tie with their own children: They cannot understand why people from their parents' generation, who grew up in the intense Jewish families of eastern European ghettos, were so concerned about their children.

The founders of the kibbutz movement were influenced by the radical post-Freudian ideologies popular early in the twentieth century, and they deliberately wanted to weaken the family in order to eliminate the Oedipus complex and the adolescent identity crisis. They assigned all education and discipline to *metapelets* and teachers, because they thought it was important for parents to have only good times with their children and to avoid conflicts over discipline. The kibbutz would avoid these conflicts by separating love from discipline.[83]

Children know that the important decisions about their lives are made by the kibbutz education committee, not by their parents. This does reduce conflict, as it was meant to, but it also makes the relationship between parent and child more shallow. Bettelheim heard arguments between parents and children on the kibbutz that began as personal disagreements, with the parents forbidding the child to do something, but that quickly turned impersonal when both child and parents realized that the kibbutz collective itself forbade what the child wanted to do.[84] By contrast, among the American middle class, the parents get the blame for forbidding these sorts of activities, although they are not really as powerful as their children think. On the kibbutz, even very young children realize that their parents do not make the rules, and

> the knowledge that all decisions of importance are not made by the parents . . . makes the parent seem less formidable but also a bit less of a person. . . . Thinking then of how the young child sees his parents in society, the middle-class parent appears more self-determined, powerful, and hence dangerous, but for the same reasons more of a person.[85]

In this situation, children develop a conscience not by internalizing the authority of parents but by internalizing the kibbutz's collective rules. Doing what is right is no different from doing what is practical, what is necessary to get along in the kibbutz environment: In the Freudian terms that Bettelheim uses, the superego can hardly be distinguished from the ego among kibbutz children.[86] As a result, children growing up on the kibbutz are very well adjusted and rarely have psychological problems, because struggles with their conscience over what is right and wrong do not get in the way of doing what is practical to get on the world.

Yet these children pay for their adjustment when they reach adolescence and fail to develop a strong sense of self. A conscience that comes from internalizing individual authority figures, such as parents, can make people feel that they must stand up against the group; sometimes they even change the group.[87] But children who grow up on the kibbutz cannot even understand why someone would stand up against the community in this way. Ideas and ideals mean very little to them.

At debates in the kibbutz general assembly, there was a stark contrast between the founding generation and the people who were born on the kibbutz. The founders and those who moved onto the kibbutz as adults argued with gusto and enjoyed the ideas for their own sake, apart from the practical results of the debate. The kibbutz-born were self-assured but uninterested in ideas.[88] Likewise, the first generation often read several newspapers to get diverse opinions, even though they believed firmly in their own leftist politics. The kibbutz-born, by contrast, read widely but avoided publications containing any opinions but their own: They read professional publications in their own fields and, when it came to politics, they just read the party newspaper, hearing about other opinions only as they were described there.[89]

The founders of the kibbutz movement were idealistic intellectuals: They believed they were "the carrier of great new ideas, a brighter future."[90] By contrast, those who were born on the kibbutz saw it as a practical, expedient way of life; their matter-of-factness had no place for idealism.[91] The second generation, born on the kibbutz of parents who came from eastern Europe, made fun of what they called their parents' "great ideas." The third generation, those born of parents who were born on the kibbutz, did not care at all about their grandparents' great ideas.[92]

The founders agonized over whether they were establishing the best methods for educating their children, but the kibbutz-born did not share this concern. As one founder said: "We brought up our children with such careful consideration for them as human beings, but when they grow up and work as nurses, even those who have children of their own, they are much less concerned."[93] For their part, the kibbutz-born complained that the older generation of nurses, *metapelets*, and teachers were too involved personally, that they should have considered the work of raising children to be the same as any other work assignment.[94]

Despite these problems, Bettelheim concluded that the kibbutz was a mixed success. He was disturbed by this shallowness of character, but as a psychologist, he was also very impressed that kibbutz-raised children were very well adjusted and almost entirely free of neuroses. The psychological mechanisms that make for greater individuality have their risks: Children raised on the kibbutz did not have an identity crisis when they reached adolescence, and as a result, none of them established a strongly individualized identity—but, on the other hand, none of them ended up believing that life is merely absurd. In some ways, the kibbutz-born reverted to the less individualized sort of character common among premodern peoples, who also raised their children in groups. Bettelheim concluded that the kibbutz is one worthwhile element in Israeli society: "While such people do not create science or art, are neither leaders nor great philosophers nor innovators, maybe it is they who are the salt of the earth without whom no society can endure."[95]

It would be much more worrisome if this sort of character were not just one element of society but instead became the dominant social character. Yet studies of the changing American national character during the twentieth century suggest that a similar sort of character has started to become dominant here as our child-raising methods have changed.

THE LONELY CROWD

One of the earliest and most influential studies of the changing American character was David Riesman's 1950 book *The Lonely Crowd*, which puts modern America in a broader historical perspective by looking at three different types of society that Riesman called tradition-directed, inner-directed, and other-directed. This schema helps to explain how changes in child-raising methods are connected to larger economic and social changes.

Most premodern cultures are tradition-directed. Because their economies and social organization change slowly, people can follow traditional patterns of behavior that have always been proper for those of their age, sex, or caste. Each person has a defined relationship to the group and to other people, and there are relatively fixed rules of conduct that govern the important activities of life, such as courtship, work, child-raising, and religion.[96] In the Middle Ages, for example, people worked the land in the same way and followed the same religious ceremonies generation after generation; what you did with your life was determined by whether you were born peasant or noble, man or woman.

The inner-directed character appeared when economic changes made these old rules of conduct obsolete. This happened in classical Greece, and it happened again at the end of the late Middle Ages. The urban economies that emerged at these times were very different from the traditional economies of the countryside and were more dynamic. The traditional rules of conduct no longer applied in societies that were changing so rapidly.

The Renaissance in southern Europe and the Reformation in northern and western Europe created a more individualistic character, less bound by old rules and rituals. Despite their differences, Riesman says, the new forms of character that emerged at the time all had one thing in common: "The source of direction for the individual is 'inner' . . . implanted early in life by the elders and directed toward generalized but nonetheless inescapably destined goals."[97] In a changing society, there can no longer be detailed rules of behavior that tell each person what to do: People cannot decide how to act by thinking about how a peasant always behaved or how a noblewoman always behaved. Instead, people had a strong inner commitment to general goals—such as obeying God's will, pursuing knowledge, or making money—that gave them a direction when they faced new situations.

In modern technological economies, this inner-directed character has been replaced by the other-directed character, as small businesses run by individuals were replaced by corporate bureaucracies that require people to get along well with a group. These bureaucracies must deal with consumers to keep them buying their products and must deal with workers to keep them happy and efficient. The objective difficulties of material production are less important than the psychological difficulties of human relations.

In this situation, a new type of character is needed that is attuned to other people. The other-directed live in a rapidly changing economy and constantly encounter new situations, but rather than being guided by inner principles that they believe in, they look to the peer group for direction—to peers they know directly, and peers they have heard about through friends or the mass media.[98]

Child-Raising

Riesman is very clear about the different methods of child-raising that tend to create these types of social character.

In tradition-directed societies, children are raised by the extended family, tribe, or clan. Because the skills needed by adults do not change over the generations and do not require formal education, children can learn by watching and helping the adults who are around them. Different age groups are not separated: Children spend their days with adults while they perform ordinary economic activities, they learn to imitate their elders, and they ultimately take their places. This form of child-raising leaves little room for individualism: Children grow up into the traditional economic activities and conventional social roles that surround them.

In inner-directed societies, new frontiers are being explored economically and intellectually, so children can not simply imitate their parents' roles when they grow up. Instead, they need a character committed to general ideals and goals so strongly that they can deal with demanding new tasks without ever losing sight of their purpose.[99] In tradition-directed families, parents usually just keep children from being a nuisance, and they often have older sisters take care of them; as long as the children's behavior is not a bother, they are content. But inner-directed parents deliberately try to build their children's characters.[100]

Parents can work on their children's characters because they have much more authority over children than before and because the extended family has less influence.[101] The one-room house of the peasant's extended family or the castle of the noble extended family gave way to a separate home for the immediate family, with separate rooms for parents and children. It first became common for people to move to their own homes after they married, rather than staying in the household of their extended family, in northwestern Europe (particularly England, France, and the low countries) at the end of the Middle Ages, and historians have argued that this change led to the rise of individualism in these countries and ultimately to the ideals of the American and French Revolutions.

Children not only had a more intense relationship with their parents; they also had privacy for the first time, so they could think in solitude about their conversations with their parents. After arguing with parents who were trying to develop their characters, they could continue the conflicts in their own rooms as internal arguments in their own minds,[102] creating what Riesman calls "an individual with an historically new level of self-awareness."[103] After they have grown up, they feel that they must continue working on their characters throughout their lives.

Riesman concludes that the inner-directed character appeared because parents had more say in building their children's characters and because children's increased privacy promoted inner dialogue and self-awareness—exactly the same points that Bettelheim makes about the "middle-class American children" whom he contrasts with kibbutz-born children.

The other-directed character has appeared because the economy is still dynamic and changing, and people have to compete for their place in it, but now they need personality to succeed rather than character: "Parents who try, in inner-directed fashion, to compel the internalization of disciplined pursuit of clear goals run the risk of having their children styled clear out of the personality market."[104] Instead, children are educated in schools, surrounded by the peer group. In modern societies, children and adolescents are the first ones to pick up the latest fashions, and parents imitate the new styles that children learn from their peers and the mass media.

Schooling

Among the inner-directed, schooling "starts relatively late,"[105] Riesman says—not at the nursery school level—and teachers have little interest in the emotional life of the children. Schools enforce basic rules of morality and teach some formal manners, ranging from the social polish that girls pick up in finishing school to the middle-class manners and speech that immigrants learn in public schools, but these manners have a certain impersonality to them. Teachers have not studied child psychology, and the school's main focus is on intellectual skills rather than on the child's personality.[106] Everyone takes it for granted that the school's academic standards are objectively valid and that it is up to the children to live up to these standards.

Progressive education changed all this during the twentieth century, as our society became more other-directed: "The two- to five-year-old groups learn to associate school not with forbidding adults and dreary subjects but with play and understanding adults . . . who have been taught to be more concerned with the child's social and psychological adjustment than with his academic progress."[107] Schoolteachers are trained in special teachers colleges, where the courses focus on educational psychology rather than on grammar, mathematics, and other academic subjects. The formal seating of old-fashioned public schools, where children were arranged in alphabetical order, is replaced with informal seating in progressive schools, as teachers try to divide the class to place the children in the proper peer groups. Children are promoted automatically, regardless of whether they have mastered the subject matter, so that they can stay with their peer group; the school is willing to bend its academic standards on the grounds that enforcing them might harm the children psychologically, because its focus is therapeutic rather than intellectual.[108]

Activities that would have been private in earlier generations are socialized by the schools. For example, old-fashioned schools made sure that students read the books that were assigned by giving them exams that required them to identify the books' characters or describe their plots; as long as you did the reading and knew these basic facts, you were left to like or dislike the book in your own way. By contrast, progressive schools have their students write and talk about why they enjoyed the book. Because the appreciation that used to be private is now open to everyone, there is pressure to make your taste conform to everyone else's.

The Peer Group

The child's relation to the peer group also changes when we move from an inner-directed to an other-directed society.

Inner-directed children play with other children of a wide range of ages; the kids who live and play on the same city block all know each other, regardless of age. When they approach their teens, inner-directed children usually seek out one or two close friends, often on the basis of common interests in games or hobbies. When Riesman wrote, this was still common at English boys' schools, where almost all the children had hobbies, some quite idiosyncratic—such as bird watching, rock collecting, or reading and writing poetry—that they indulged in by themselves and that sometimes became the basis of close friendships.[109] Some children were lonely and isolated, and the peer group tormented some children, as they always do in books about the English public schools; but as painful as these things can be, Riesman says, we now "can see that in a society which values inner-direction loneliness and even persecution are not thought of as the worst of fates. Parents, sometimes even teachers, may have crushing moral authority, but the peer-group has less moral weight."[110] Adults probably will not step in to help a child who is persecuted by the peer group; but they also will not tell the child that it is wrong not to get along with the peer group.

By contrast, other-directed children—at school, at summer camp, or in organized games—play almost exclusively with other children of the same age. The child, Riesman says, is surrounded by the peer group but "is not surrounded by those who are his peers in less visible matters, such as temperament and taste. Yet since there are no *visible* differences, he is hard put to it to justify, even to be aware of, these *invisible differences.*"[111] Rather than developing tastes of one's own, especially if they are idiosyncratic, children are expected to be interested in whatever is the current fashion among children of their age.

Adolescent rebellion itself has changed dramatically because of this change in character type. Rebellious youth used to reject conventional ideas to decide for themselves what is the best way to live: Thoreau is the archetype in America. But by the 1950s, adolescents rebelled by joining a rebellious peer group (such as the beats or the hippies) and following its fashions in hairstyle, dress, and slang.

The peer group constantly invents new words to enforce its tastes. In the 1950s, it decided some things were "cool" and others were "square." That was the first time that words invented to express the judgments of the adolescent peer group became the common currency of society as a whole, and teenagers since then have kept inventing new words that mean the same thing. It is hard for an individual to resist the peer group, because it enforces conformity through judgments that are matters of taste, not of morality.[112] Back when the other adolescents said that you were wrong, you could resist if you genuinely believed you were right, but it is much harder to resist when the other kids say they are all hip and you are a dork.

LOVE AND DISCIPLINE

Riesman thought the sensitive other-directed character was better in many ways than the rigid inner-directed character, and he complained that people misinterpreted his book and thought he meant inner-direction was better than other-direction.[113] But after the changes he described had gone further, it became clear that the people who misinterpreted Riesman were right. He was describing the beginning of a real decline in the American character. In 1969, Riesman himself admitted that he had been too optimistic: During the upheavals of the 1960s, it seemed that the well-adjusted other-directed character who always fit into the group was being replaced by an anomic character who refused to adjust to the group and who also was incapable of self-control.[114]

Changes in child-raising have gone much further since Riesman first wrote about other-direction. He described parents who used psychology to manipulate their child but were tempted, when the child argued, to fall back on the authoritarian methods that their own parents used.[115] Even this therapeutic style of parenthood has become much less common since the 1950s, because parents have much less time for their children.

By the 1970s, Christopher Lasch wrote, parents' authority had declined so drastically that there was a complete "separation of love from discipline" in the typical American family. Lasch said that parents presented "themselves to their children strictly as older friends and companions," while "the school, the helping professions, and the peer group have taken over most of the family's functions."[116] The parents' role has become so weak that most American children, like children who grow up on the kibbutz, do not internalize their parents' authority in the form of a conscience.[117] Just as people raised on the kibbutz act on the basis of expediency rather than of ideals, people raised in modern America submit to the rules of social life, Lasch said, "because submission usually represents the line of least resistance, not because they believe in the justice of the rules."[118]

America and the Kibbutz

In fact, when we think about Bettelheim's contrast between kibbutz and "middle-class American" methods of raising children, we cannot help being shocked by how suddenly our child-raising methods have changed. Today, just a few decades after Bettelheim wrote, most middle-class American children are raised in a way that is more like his description of the kibbutz than his description of the American middle class.

For example, Bettleheim says that middle-class infants spend their days watching their parents or in solitude, while kibbutz infants are constantly surrounded by many people and lack solitude, which makes them less capable of intimacy when they grow up. Today's infants in day care are much more like the children of the kibbutz than they are like old-fashioned middle-class children. They spend most of their time with their peers rather with than their parents, and they lack solitude.

Bettelheim says that life on the kibbutz is dominated by the peer group and lacks real intimacy. In 1950, Riesman already saw that the peer group was becoming more important to American teenagers than the one or two close friends that adolescents had searched for in the past, and dating often had nothing to do with intimacy. Today, teenagers are just as immersed in the peer group as they were in the 1950s, and even among adults, marriage sometimes seems no deeper than the shallow, shifting friendships of teenagers.

Decisions about how kibbutz children are raised are made by the education committee, while American parents still have formal authority over their children. But in 1950, Riesman already saw that parents had lost much of their real authority to the schools and the peer group. Many decisions about child-raising are made by the education bureaucracy—and the bureaucracy would take over completely if we took the final step of providing federally funded day care.

Parents on the kibbutz are officially restricted to a 2-hour visit, while American parents live with their children. But most working parents with long commutes spend less than 2 hours a day with their preschool children. As day care became common during the 1970s, everyone began to talk about "quality time"—and here, too, they sound like parents on the kibbutz, who "try to crowd too much emotion into the short span of time, because they feel the visit comprises the whole of their relations with their children. They want it to be so good and so meaningful."[119] Since parents are trying so hard during these visits, the one thing that they cannot do is relax and be themselves.

Quality time also takes away children's last chance for solitude: They spend all day interacting with their peers, and then they must spend the evening interacting intensely with their parents. Bettelheim usually says that middle-class American children have more than enough solitude,[120] but, on occasion, he admits that American life was changing as he wrote and that children were losing their solitude.[121] If anything, the lack of solitude and silence is worse in America than it is on the kibbutz, because the mass media are so pervasive here. People on the kibbutz are often out in nature by themselves during their work, but Americans are more likely to enjoy nature by taking a drive in the country, with the car radio jabbering the whole time.

Like the children of the kibbutz, today's Americans are motivated not by ideals but by expediency. Most philosophers and most ordinary people no longer believe there is an objective morality that can be known by reason or conscience. Inner-directed people submitted to rules that they believed were right; they at least invented a rationalization, however hypocritical, to persuade themselves that the rules were right; and they sometimes disobeyed the rules to follow a higher authority. But many modern Americans obey the rules when it is to their advantage, and are just as willing to break the rules when *that* is to their advantage. In Lasch's phrase, they "submit not to authority but to reality."[122]

Yet people with this sort of character behave differently in the kibbutz and in America. Children on the kibbutz remain with the same peers all their lives, their economic opportunities are very limited, and everyone knows everyone else. By contrast, in our open society, there is more temptation to manipulate others for the sake of your own self-interest.[123]

Bettelheim says kibbutz psychology is viable in a small, closed society where there is no criticism of social arrangements, no low forms of diversion except movies once or twice a week, no property to be stolen, and no delinquent peer groups.[124] It is hard to avoid being well adjusted when society is so all-encompassing.

In any open society, though, adjustment will sometimes fail. If they have no inner source of values, people who do not fit into social roles will become anomic. They will feel that there are no rules guiding them at all, that their lives are meaningless, absurd. They are likely to turn to drugs, alcohol, or crime because they have no reason to restrain themselves from acting on impulse, self-destructively or violently.

Adjustment or Anomie

The social character of postwar America has fluctuated between adjustment and anomie. During the 1950s, adjustment was the guiding principle, though there were worries about juvenile delinquents, beatniks, and other anomic deviant groups. During the 1960s and 1970s, there was a surge of anomie: Youth culture attacked conventional morality and refused to conform to society's rules, but it did not have any higher morality to substitute for the conventional rules, so it turned to impulsive behavior, to "sex, drugs, and rock and roll."

During the 1980s and the 1990s, adjustment became popular again. For example, educational achievement improved during the 1950s, declined during 1960s and 1970s, and began to improve again during the 1980s. But the students are abandoning the liberal arts in favor of vocational majors: They are working hard because they want good jobs when they graduate— not because they consider the subjects they are studying intrinsically interesting. They are motivated by expediency: Staying in the school system and working hard is the best way to get what they want for themselves. And young people who cannot succeed in the school system find it expedient to deal drugs: That is the best way for them to get what they want for themselves.

The crime rate has decreased, but some of the crimes are more brutal than ever. Some teenage criminals seem to be totally without conscience and incapable of remorse, which was not true 50 years ago. A small number of teenagers enjoy "rat-packing" or "wilding"—random attacks on strangers with no motive beyond the joy of violence—and large numbers of teenagers enjoy slasher movies, gangsta rap, and "death metal" rock music, the subgenre of heavy metal rock whose lyrics graphically describe murder and torture.[125] Most adolescents are adjusted, as they were in the 1950s, but the anomic groups are frightening; the beatniks and juvenile delinquents of the 1950s look innocent by comparison.

Adjustment and anomie go together. They are the two possibilities for people who lack any inner source of values.

When Riesman wrote, the decline of the inner-directed character seemed to fit right in with the needs of the technological economy of postwar America, but now that this change has gone further, it seems much more problematic for a society to lose the sense that there is an objective moral order. Liberals want more therapeutic organizations to deal with these new social problems: It is conceivable that they could succeed and create a society where people are all well adjusted, but only if they are willing to create a society as all-encompassing and total as the kibbutz—a society where all the infants are in day-care centers, all the children are in schools and after-school programs, and all the adolescents are tracked directly from school into nine-to-five jobs. In this sort of society, people would be happy in their social roles: The way they were raised would leave them free from inner debates about right and wrong, which might stop them from acting in a realistic, expedient way.

NEEDED RESEARCH

So far, there is only anecdotal evidence to show that adults who were in day care as infants have the sort of character that we would expect.

"Karen" was placed in day care as an infant during the 1950s, when it was still uncommon. During the 1970s, she went through a period of rebellion against her parents and conventional values, like many of her friends, but unlike her friends, she did not become involved in idealistic political causes. Instead, she majored in psychology and talked endlessly about her "relationships." After she dropped out of graduate school, Karen spent a couple of years living unconventionally and working at low-paying, part-time jobs, and then she decided that she would do best by studying computer programming. She was happy that she could coast through junior college computer courses without much work, because they were not intellectually demanding, and after two years, she was hired as an entry-level programmer by the country's largest bank. She has been working nine-to-five for large corporations ever since. When you first meet her, you cannot tell how little ideals and ideas mean to her: She is intelligent enough that she can use ideas as topics of conversation, in order to get along with other people. You have to know her well before you realize that she is not interested in ideas for their own sake, and she cannot even imagine that an idea could change someone's behavior. She and her boyfriend decided not to have any children, because, as she once said without any suspicion that her attitude was unusual, "having children would make it harder for us to go out to movies and restaurants."

To go beyond this sort of anecdotal evidence and come to real conclusions about the psychological effects of day care, we need in-depth studies of American adults who are similar socioeconomically, except that some were put in day care at a very early age while others stayed at home until they started elementary school. It is possible to conduct this sort of study now, for the first time, because both of these options were common by the 1970s, and the children born then are now adults. These studies would have to be done by people who have a broad view of history and culture, like Riesman and Bettelheim: It takes people who are humanists, as well as a social scientists, to see whether adults who were raised in day-care centers have the well-adjusted but empty character that we would expect.

But the psychologists who study day care have not even looked at this question. Instead, they have prolonged debates about very narrow issues.

For example, there have been fierce disputes over studies based on "attachment theory," where psychologists observe the behavior of infants to see whether they are securely or insecurely attached to their mothers. The psychologist Jay Belsky claimed these studies showed that infants of less than 1 year old who are in day care more than 20 hours a week are insecure. This modest conclusion provoked a storm of criticism from day-care advocates.[126] But the most striking thing about this debate is how narrow it is. Psychologists focus on secure and insecure attachment only because it is easy to observe this behavior among infants. Attachment theory gives researchers a technique that lets them do experiments and come up with quantitative results—but that does not mean this technique looks at the most important effects of day care.

Attachment theory was popularized as the idea of "bonding"—the idea that it is essential to bond with an infant during the first months of life, implying that you can then leave the rest of your child's upbringing to the day-care centers and schools—and the public seemed to accept the idea that bonding is all-important, just because it is the easiest thing for psychologists to study empirically.

The press reports these studies as if they were definitive. For example, one recent study by the National Institute for Child Health and Human Development found that children thrive if they have a rich and stimulating environment, whether it is provided at home or at a day-care center. This study claimed to be larger and more detailed than any earlier study, because it had 10 teams of researchers studying 1,300 families across the country—but it only studied these children from birth to age 7. A study that does not go beyond age 7 would also find that kibbutz child-raising methods have little psychological effect on children, except that kibbutz children are likely to be well adjusted. Yet newspapers reported this study on the front page, under headlines reading: "No Harm In Day Care, Study Says."[127]

Our experts do not even know what questions to ask. American psychologists today do not get the broad classical education that was common when Bettelheim was young, and they do not even know that they should be looking for the sort of thing that Bettelheim saw on the kibbutz: people who are free from the mental health problems that they learned about in their psychology classes, who are happy and very well adjusted, but who lack human depth.

4

LEGISLATION FOR
OUR CHILDREN

TIME TO GO SLOW

Most child-care advocates argue that we must provide day care, whether we want to or not, because most mothers now have to work. When studies show that day care might be harmful—like Jay Belsky's studies in attachment theory, which found that full-time day care might harm children under 1 year old—child-care advocates go on the defensive and answer that there is "no conclusive evidence" that day care causes psychological damage to children.

It is unlikely that there will be conclusive evidence about the psychological effects of day care for decades, since researchers have not even begun to ask the key questions about day care and social character.

The researchers also have political biases that make it harder for them to find the truth about day care. In fact, the most celebrated expert on the subject, Benjamin Spock, admitted that he concealed his opinions about day care:

> I'm scared of going out too strongly for "You should stay home!" because in the early editions of *Baby and Child Care*, I hinted at that by saying "The early years are very crucial, and maybe you should postpone the advantages of

earning a living." And women pounced on me, they said, "You made me feel very guilty!" but I noticed they went off to work anyway, even if they felt guilty, and that's . . . the worst of all possible arrangements! So I just tossed it. It's a cowardly thing that I did, I just tossed it in subsequent editions.[128]

Instead, Spock decided, "if you had ideal day care, the repercussions wouldn't be so bad,"[129] and so he started campaigning for more funding for day-care centers.

What should our policy be if there is no conclusive evidence that high-quality day care causes psychological damage? Does it follow that we should spend billions of dollars to provide higher-quality day care, since it probably causes less damage than low-quality day care?

If no one knows what the psychological effects of day care are, we should at least develop policies that are cautious.

The use of day care has increased at a frightening rate. As recently as the mid 1960s, it was considered so odd to take infants out of the home that most states with legislation regulating day care refused even to license facilities for children under 3 years old.[130] Today, the majority of children under 3 are cared for outside of their homes. If we react by spending even more money to provide high-quality day care, there will be an entire generation of children raised in day care before we know its effects on social character. By the time there is "conclusive evidence" that day care is harmful, it will be too late to do anything about it.

FAMILY AND DAY CARE

If we are uncertain about the effects of day care, we should adopt it more slowly than we have in the past few decades. Rather than spending more to subsidize day care, we should eliminate the obvious forms of discrimination against families who take care of their own preschool children, so that fewer people will need to use day care.

Child-Care Tax Credits

As a first step, we need to reform the child-care tax credit, to increase the support it gives to parents and also to include parents who work shorter hours to take care of their own children.

Currently, this federal income tax credit goes to all families with children in day care, from the poorest to the wealthiest, and to no one else. The is one of the most widely used tax credits, amounting to $2.5 billion for child care and other dependent care.[131] It goes largely to upper-income families: Families with incomes in the top 30 percent take half of the child-care tax credits, and those in the bottom 30 percent get only 3 percent of these credits.[132] Dual-income families get most of these benefits; families with much lower incomes who take care of their own children at home get nothing.[133]

We could make the tax credit fairer by offering it to families with preschool-age children where the spouses work less than, say, 50 hours a week combined. Families that take off this much time to care for their own children are making a much greater financial sacrifice than two-income families that pay for full-time day care.

Since aid should be based on need, this credit should be refundable, so low-income families can take full advantage of it; and it should be available to low- and moderate-income families, but not to high-income families.

Increasing this tax credit until it is enough to pay the full cost of high-quality day care is the most important thing we can do to help parents who need day care as well as parents who want to care for their own children.

Child-care advocates always demand direct government funding for high-quality day-care centers, but they do not mention that giving this funding directly to families with preschool children would let most of them to do without day care. According to one study, high-quality day care costs $9,000 per child;[134] demonstration programs of high-quality day care cost as much as $11,000 per child.[135] By comparison, the median after-tax income of women who work full time is less than $20,000.[136] When you take into account the cost of commuting, lunches, clothing, and maybe also a second car, the second job nets $10,000 to $15,000—not much more than the cost of putting one preschool child in high-quality day care, and much less than the cost of putting two preschool children in high-quality day care.

Most moderate-income couples who are now driven by financial need to work an 80-hour week would be able to take care of their own children if we funded child care by giving a tax credit to parents of preschool children rather than providing the massive subsidies for day care that child-care advocates demand.

Single parents and other low-income people who need day care would be no worse off than they are now, since they could use this credit to pay for day care. In fact, they would be better off than they would be under the usual liberal proposals for government-funded day care, since they would be able to choose the day care themselves rather than being forced into the programs that the government funds.

Since we know so little about the psychological effects of day care, it is essential that we go slow by funding child care in a way that preserves a diversity of child-raising methods. That is exactly what this sort of tax credit does, by giving families the choice of putting their children in day care full time, putting their preschool children in part-time programs to supplement their child care at home, or raising their preschool children full time in their homes and neighborhoods.

Minnesota is the first state to help stay-at-home parents as well as parents using day care. In 1994, Minnesota passed the At-Home Child Care Credit Bill, which gives a tax credit of $720 per child (for up to two children) to married couples who care for their babies at home during the first year of life; and in 1998, it added the At-Home Infant Child Care Bill, which gives parents who provide full-time care for an infant child subsidies equal to 75 percent of the rate for infant day care.[137] These laws are a small first step in the right direction.

Politically, it would be much easier to provide nondiscriminatory child-care tax credits than to provide funding for day-care centers. If the Democratic party shifted its emphasis and started campaigning for a larger child-care tax credits, with most benefits going to low- and moderate-income families, it would be very difficult for the Republicans to oppose bills that helped more parents to care for their own children. This approach is the most politically practical way to get more funding for child care.

Corporate Child Care Inc.

In addition to demanding massive funding for day care from the federal government, child-care advocates have turned to the private sector, which has been fairly responsive.

The country is more likely to be blanketed with chains of privately managed day-care centers than with government managed day-care centers. Leading the way is Kinder-Care Inc., which runs more than 1,100 day-care centers in 38 states, nationwide, with a "curriculum developed by our on-staff Ph.D. specialists" and "state-of-the-art facilities."[138] Americans seem to consume this sort of standard mass commodity without thinking: It has not come to this yet, but eventually people may put their children in day-care chains without thinking about whether their programs are good, just as they feed their children at McDonald's without thinking about whether their food is healthy.

The most progressive employers provide on-site day care, which makes parents even more powerless than big day-care chains. You can move your child to a different chain if you think there is something wrong with the one you are using, but most people could not afford to do anything about it if they thought there was something wrong with the way their corporate day-care center was raising their children. This is the most rapidly growing form of day care: In 1995 alone, the number of companies offering on-site day care increased by 25 percent.[139]

In what may be a foretaste of the future, the developers of the Hacienda Business Park in northern California spent $3.2 million on what they described as "a state-of-the-art child-care center, complete with incandescent lighting, heated floors, and a lounge for the staff," which is used by employees of AT&T and the other corporations that lease space at this complex. The developers considered the child-care center a major selling point that would help them get tenants. As one said, "If child-care can bond an employee to his or her employer, then that bonding is going on between the employer and the developer of the park."[140]

The state of California now requires most state office buildings to have on-site child care. San Francisco, Berkeley, and other progressive California cities require private developers either to provide child care on-site or to pay a fee into a city fund used to build day-care centers. In fact, there is a California company, named "Corporate Child Care Inc.," which contracts with developers to run their on-site child-care centers.

This sounds like the latest version of the California dream. After spending the weekend at the mall, you can start the week by driving on the freeway to "Hacienda Business Park" and leaving your 3-month-old baby at a "state-of-the-art" child-care center.

Federal tax laws also encourage corporations to subsidize day care. In addition to the child-care tax credit, the tax laws allow employers to provide up to $5,000 in child-care benefits tax-free. Employers can provide on-site day-care services without their value being counted as taxable income. If they do not provide child-care themselves, they can shelter the income employees use to pay for day care from taxes.[141] Of course, there is no equivalent tax benefit for parents who take care of their own children.

Like the child-care tax credit, this tax law is blatantly discriminatory. It encourages businesses to give extra benefits to parents who use day care and to give nothing to parents who raise their own children. Instead of passing laws that encourage this sort of discrimination, we should pass strict laws that forbid it. Any business that provides day-care benefits should provide equivalent benefits to employees with preschool-age children who live on a single income or work shorter hours in order to take care of their own children.

The push to have businesses provide on-site child care could destroy the livelihoods of many older people who earn a bit of money by taking care of their grandchildren and a couple of other young children. It could be devastating to families who earn extra money by taking care of a neighbor's child along with their own: Many of them could not afford to take care of their own children at home without the extra income they get from caring for a neighbor's child, and the spread of corporate child care could force them into the ranks of working parents searching for day care themselves.

If we want to strengthen families, we have to stop encouraging people to put their children in the sort of institutional day care that makes parents most powerless. As a first step, we need to fund all child care in a way that is nondiscriminatory, that gives parents the choice of how their own children are raised.

Educating the Public

In addition to creating a level playing field by ending discrimination against parents who care for their own children, we should educate parents about the importance of raising their own preschool children.

Studies have shown that children are more successful in school if adults talk to them, sing to them, read to them, and have repeated affectionate interactions with them when they are infants—beginning before they have learned to speak. Most middle-class parents already do this, but many low-income parents do not talk and read to their infant children.

We could improve child-raising dramatically with a large-scale public education campaign, like the campaign about the dangers of smoking, to let all parents know that they can help their preschool children by doing these simple things.

Unfortunately, the studies that could be used to help parents have been used instead to undermine parents' confidence in their ability to raise their own children. The latest example is the Abecedarian Project, which is used to argue that high-quality day care does better than the family: Even the usually staid (and accurate) *New York Times* reported on it under the head-line "Quality Day Care, Early, Is Tied to Achievement as an Adult." This sort of thing has led many middle-class parents to believe that they should put their children in day-care centers to provide them with an enriched environment.

In reality, the Abecedarian Project enrolled only low-income, at-risk children, and what it did for them was no different from what most middle-class parents already do: Read to them, talked to them, sang to them, held them, and gave them interesting toys to play with. As a result, the poor, at-risk children who entered this program at the age of 4 months did better than the control group of at-risk children who stayed home, but they still did much worse than the average American child. For example, 30 percent of the children in the Abecedarian program had to repeat a year in school, compared with 56 percent of the control group who stayed home, and IQ scores of children in the program were 5 points higher at age 21 than those of children in the control group. In both cases, the children did better than they would have if they had not been in this program, but they still did far worse than the average child.[142]

It is not surprising that the benefits were so small, since studies have shown that differences in quality of day care account for only 1 to 4 percent of the differences in children's scores in tests of cognitive development, while the rest can be attributed to differences among their families.[143]

We can obviously do much more to help these children by supporting and educating their families than by putting them in day-care centers. The Abecedarian Project concluded that poor families need day care only because it started out by assuming that poor parents are too dumb to raise their own children, so it never even tested the possibility of educating parents. There seems to be a racist subtext here: More than 95 percent of the parents they chose to study and declared to be incompetent were African Americans.

Unfortunately, day-care advocates have mystified parents by confusing this sort of program with studies showing that animals' brains do not develop properly if they are deprived of stimulation during critical periods of their infancy. For example, if kittens have one eye covered during infancy, they are never able to see in that eye after it is uncovered, because their brains have not developed the necessary synapses, so day-care advocates claim that children will be "hard-wired" to succeed in school if they are put in enriched environments when they are infants. Yet the experiments they cite apply only to traits that are common to the entire species, such as vision. Other experiments have shown that there are not critical periods for developing culturally specific traits, such as the ability to read. Most important, the experiments they cite only show that animals require normal stimulation to develop these normal capabilities, not that there is any benefit to especially enriched environments. It has been shown that children's brains will not develop properly if they are deprived of normal stimulation, for example, if no one talks to them at all during infancy. But brain science has not reached the point where it knows whether especially enriched environments can help the brain develop—and it certainly does not know how to create these enriched environments.

In fact, if you look at the literature of groups such as Rob Reiner's We Are Your Children, you will find that they begin with a brief discussion of brain science to give their ideas scientific credibility, and then go on to call for day-care programs that provide "enriched environments" by doing exactly what most middle-class parents already do—talking to infants long before they have learned to speak, reading to them, singing to them, giving them interesting toys to play with, having affectionate interactions with them.

You do not need a degree in brain science to do these things. We could improve child-raising dramatically if we mounted a large-scale public education campaign with television advertisements and billboards to show everyone how important they are.

The effect could be as dramatic as the improvement in public health in the 1970s and 1980s, when the rate of heart disease dropped sharply because of widespread public education telling people that they would be healthier if they cut down on smoking, ate less fat, and exercised more. Health improved dramatically when we spread the word that people should do more to protect their own health, and child care will improve dramatically when we spread the word that people should do more for their own preschool children.

What we need is a change in our thinking. Parents began to send their children to kindergarten and nursery schools in the early twentieth century because they had faith in programs designed by developmental psychologists. Parents will stop sending their children to day care when they have more faith in themselves.

FAMILY AND SCHOOLING

Child-raising does not stop after children move from preschool to school age. We also need to strengthen the family to improve education: The research shows that quality of family and community life are the key factors influencing academic achievement.

Family and Academic Success

Early in the twentieth century, educators had great faith in preschools and schools, but during the past few decades, the largest-scale and most important studies on educational achievement have shown that a child's home and community have much more effect than the quality of schooling.

During the 1960s, the federally funded Coleman Report, *Equality of Educational Opportunity*, found that quality of schooling accounted for very little of the difference in achievement between students at different schools. Differences in achievement among schools were caused largely by socioeconomic differences among their students[144]; when socioeconomic factors were statistically controlled for, differences among schools still accounted for only about 10 percent of the difference in achievement.[145] For example, Coleman found that parents were twice as important as schools to children's achievement at age 14.[146]

During the 1970s, there was another major, federally funded study of the subject, run by Christopher Jencks, which concluded that "qualitative differences between schools had relatively little impact on students' test scores . . . differences between schools also have relatively little effect on students' eventual educational attainment."[147] Instead, Jencks's statistical analysis showed "that the most important determinant of educational attainment is family background."[148]

Many other studies have made the same point: Spending more and reducing class size have little or no effect on educational achievement, but family and community *do* matter.[149]

Unfortunately, though Coleman's and Jencks's studies were considered authoritative during the 1960s and 1970s, they had no practical effect. The divorce rate was soaring, and parents had less time and attention to devote to their children. Liberals were saying that you had to be "pragmatic" and spend more on child care and schooling, as if the family were dispensable as long as you spent enough money.

Although the amount we spend on schooling soared during the 1960s and 1970s, educational achievement declined dramatically.[150] During the 1980s a national commission found that, for the first time in our history, we had produced a generation of students who were less well educated than their parents.[151] As a reaction to this decline, there was a conservative reform movement that insisted on back-to-basics teaching and higher academic standards. But when the Carnegie Foundation surveyed more than 13,500 teachers to assess the effects of school reform, its findings confirmed that students' families were more of a problem than their schools.[152] The overwhelming majorities of the teachers who were interviewed said that some children they had to deal with were undernourished, abused, or neglected at home. The president of the Carnegie Foundation summed up the report by saying that most teachers say students are "emotionally needy" and "starved for affection," and:

> Today's parents have less time to engage in the educational progress of their children, and the role of parents in improving American education is an issue the school reform movement has largely overlooked. Teachers repeatedly made the point that in the push for better schools they cannot do the job alone, and yet there is a growing trend to expect schools to do what families, communities, and churches have been unable to accomplish.[153]

Recent studies of school reform make the same point. For example, in the most comprehensive study of high school students to date, Lawrence Steinberg and other researchers surveyed 20,000 ninth- to twelfth-grade students and their families for 1 to 3 years. They found that the quality of schooling has a significant but small effect on students' achievement and that parents and the peer group have by far the greatest effect, as earlier studies had shown. They also found that, in at least 25 percent of all American families, parents are totally disengaged from their children: They do not know how their children are doing in school, what classes they are taking, who their friends are, or how they spend their spare time; they do not even talk to their children every day.[154] Steinberg concluded that "the school reform movement has been focusing on the wrong things. The problem isn't the schools; it's the disengagement of parents and a peer culture that demeans academic performance."[155]

Hundreds of studies of child-raising during the past few decades have found that American parents fall into three groups. *Authoritarian* parents do not let their children make decisions for themselves and impose strict standards on them. *Permissive* parents let children make decisions for themselves and do not impose any standards on them. And what are called *authoritative* parents let children make decisions for themselves and also expect them to live up to high standards. These studies show conclusively that authoritative parents have the most success at raising their children, and many experts have written books advising parents that they should raise their children using the authoritative approach.

Steinberg's study confirmed that authoritative parents are most successful, but it also found that children with any of these three types of parents are far better off than children with disengaged parents. Children of disengaged parents are much more likely than any of the others to fail in school, to abuse drugs or alcohol, to commit crimes, to commit suicide, and to experience anxiety, depression, and other psychological problems.[156] There is much more of a difference between disengaged parenting and any of these three parenting styles than there is among the three styles themselves.

The experts recommend the best methods of raising children, but we have reached the point where we need to get parents involved in raising their own children and teenagers in any way at all.

Parental Control of Schooling

One thing we can do to strengthen the family's role in education is to give parents more control over their children's education through charter schools, voucher systems, magnet schools, and other forms of school choice.

In conventional public school systems, parents must send their children to the local school, and because they have no alternatives, they have no reason to think about what sort of education their children are receiving. Most parents become passive and resigned. Parents who do not fit into the mainstream, because of their political or religious beliefs, feel powerless and hostile toward the schools.

School choice gives parents more responsibility for guiding their children's schooling. This change in itself would strengthen the emotional bond between parents and children. To use Bettelheim's phrase, children would not think of their parents as "less of a person," as children on the kibbutz do, because the experts make the decisions about their education.

One common objection to school choice is that low-income parents do not have the time or information to choose schools for their children. But this claim was disproven recently, when Wall Street financier Theodore Forstmann raised $170 million for scholarships to send low-income children to private schools; students were eligible only if their income was around the cutoff level for the federal subsidized lunch program or less. The reaction: 29 percent of the eligible students in New York, 26 percent of the eligible students in Chicago, and 44 percent of the eligible children in Baltimore applied, even though the scholarship paid only half the tuition at low-cost private schools for 4 years, and parents had to pay matching contributions averaging $1,000. Though these are poor people whose children now go to public school at no cost, they turned out en masse in the hope they would have the opportunity to pay $1,000 to send their children to private schools![157]

In fact, many of the leaders of the school-choice movement are poor people who know firsthand what inner-city public schools are like.

Polly Williams was a single mother who went on and off public assistance as she raised four children, but she managed to scrimp and save enough to send her children to private elementary schools. She could not afford private high school, and when she was told in 1978 that her daughter would be bused across town, exchanging the bad neighborhood high school for a bad high school far away, she refused to be pushed around. When the school would not give her an exemption from busing, she walked into the principal's office, took the a pen and paper from his desk, and wrote a letter saying: "My daughter will stay home before I let her be bused. You may send the police to arrest me."[158] This got her the exemption, and it also made her believe more strongly than ever that ordinary people—even poor people like her—should decide how their own children are educated, rather than being controlled by social engineers with Ph.D.'s. She began a campaign for school vouchers, was elected to the Wisconsin state legislature, and put together an unusual coalition of conservatives and liberals that passed a school-choice bill in October 1989.

This bill let Milwaukee start America's first experimental school-voucher program for low-income people, which has improved children's academic achievement. A study, by a team led by Harvard professor Paul E. Peterson, compared 1,034 students using vouchers in the first 4 years of the program with 407 students who applied but were turned down for lack of space; it found that the voucher students scored 5 percentage points higher on math tests and 11 percentage points higher on reading tests—a gain equal to one-third of the gap between Black and White students nationwide, after just 4 years.[159] Yet the private schools that took vouchers spent an average of only $3,300 per student, far less than the public schools' $6,000 per student.

Milwaukee mayor John Norquist favors the voucher system because it improves achievement and also because it is essential to reversing the flight of the middle class from the cities. He says that, at first, he believed that vouchers would help students with caring parents to leave the public schools and hurt the students left behind, but then he realized the obvious fact—that middle-class students are already leaving the public schools and hurting the poor students left behind: "Instead of choosing an alternative school for their children, wealthy parents are choosing an alternative place to live, the suburbs. Vouchers would give all parents a similar power of choice, one that doesn't require moving out of town."[160] As John Norquist says, cities attract people looking for higher education because they offer the best choice of colleges; with vouchers to promote a wide choice of elementary and high schools, they could also attract people looking for K–12 schools for their children.

Oakland mayor Jerry Brown considers charter schools a key to revitalizing that city for the same reason: The middle class has fled the city to get away from its public schools. In fact, there is already a strong nationwide movement toward charter schools, which operate under a contract with the local school district—the charter—but set their own rules and hire their own employees. In 1999, there were 1,200 charter schools in 27 states, and President Clinton called for federal funding to increase the number to 3,000 in 3 years.[161]

It is estimated that 25 percent of all K–12 children already attend charter schools, private schools, magnet schools, or other alternatives to the standard public school system.[162] We can expect that school choice will continue to spread in the future.

When School Is Out

In addition to giving parents more control over schooling, we need to limit the hours of schooling to leave children some time for themselves. Solitude is not just important for preschoolers; older children and teenagers also need time for their own thoughts and their own projects. People who grow up to be serious readers, for example, virtually all begin by reading for pleasure on their own time—even though many of them disliked the books they had to read for their school assignments.

Not long ago, playing baseball with other kids on the block was an essential part of American childhood: As the children chose teams and argued about disputed plays, they learned to organize themselves and to make decisions on their own. During the nineteenth century, middle-class American children not only organized their own games; as they became older, they organized their own clubs and debating societies, which carried the competition of childhood games one step further. Long walks, alone or with one friend, were essential to adolescence—a time when people formed their own ideas.

A few decades ago, American children and teenagers had plenty of free time for play, reading, and solitude—after school got out for the day and during their long summer vacations. But today, most parents want to put their children in after-school programs and summer camps, because the only alternative is to turn them into latchkey children who go to an empty house. In these programs, the adults organize the baseball games. Rather than learning to form teams themselves, the children learn to join an organization that tells them what to do.

The modern family, where both parents work full time, is as stultifying for older children and teenagers as it is for the toddlers who are put in day care. We need to give parents more free time so they can be there for their children.

FLEXIBLE WORK HOURS

The most important change we need to give parents time for both toddlers and older children is shorter work hours and more flexible work hours. Parents should be able to arrange their schedules so that they can take care of their own infants rather than putting them in day care, so they can be home when their children get out of school rather than putting them in before- and after-school programs, and so that children can have at least part of the summer free rather than being in camp from 8 A.M. to 6 P.M. 5 days a week.

Just a few decades ago, a typical American family consisted of a father who worked full time and a mother who stayed home full time with the children.[163] If this were a reasonable world, the entry of women into the work force would have changed this so-called traditional family into a new type of family where both parents work part time and both stay at home part time. Families should not have to work longer hours overall because women work: Men and women should be able to share the work and share the time at home.

Sharing the paid work and the household work would give both men and women a more satisfying way of life than the "traditional" roles. Men in traditional families were often stultified and bored by their nine-to-five jobs, they did not have enough time to do anything serious after work, and they were cut off from the important work of raising their children. At the same time, women were stultified and bored by being stuck in the house full time, they were cut off from the larger paid economy, and they had too much responsibility for raising the children.

Family Schedules Versus Job Schedules

People should be able to fit their jobs into their families' schedules, rather than distorting their family life to fit it into the business world's nine-to-five schedule. People believe that they should put their children in day care and work full time only because we have devalued the home economy. We believe that child-raising and other work done at home is not as important as work done in the money economy. This is why we consider job schedules more important than family schedules, and this is why we have let the money economy expand so much that it crowds out the time that people used to have at home.

Now that women work as well as men, it is absurd for everyone to work the same 40-hour week that existed 50 years ago. Rather than fitting people into some sort of standard workweek, we should try make work hours as flexible as possible, so people can choose work schedules that fit their family responsibilities and their other obligations. Workers should also be allowed to take extended leave without pay, if their work flow allows it: Parental-leave legislation, which lets new parents take up to 12 weeks of unpaid leave, is a very small step in the right direction[164]; in France, the law requires businesses to give new parents up to 2 years of unpaid leave.[165]

It would not be hard to give more flexible hours to most employees. It is easy to reschedule the data-entry people in a large office, the workers in a factory, or the sales clerks at a department store. Now that businesses have computerized scheduling and recordkeeping, it is not much harder to manage 1,000 part-time clerks than it is to manage 500 full-time clerks. The extra cost of scheduling part-time workers is much less than the cost of providing day care for the children of full-time workers.

Juggling the hours of workers at smaller businesses is harder, because there are fewer people in the organization who do the same job. If an office has only two part-time workers doing data entry, there obviously has to be some compromise about the hours they work; the business could not be as flexible about their hours as a corporation where there are hundreds of people doing data entry. Rescheduling professionals is also a bit difficult, because there usually are relatively few people in any business who duplicate their skills. Yet there have been occasional experiments where people have worked part time as administrators, counselors, editors, museum designers, high school principals, librarians, and ministers.

Although not every job could offer complete flexibility, the economy could offer enough different choices to let most people find jobs with the schedules that they need.

Discrimination Against Part-Time Workers

Most people today have little or no choice of work hours because there are very few good part-time jobs. Until recently, virtually all part-time jobs were low-paid work in retail sales or services. Part-time workers still face many disadvantages: Among males, average hourly earnings of part-time workers are less than 40 percent of the hourly earnings of full-time workers, and only 15 percent of part-time workers have medical benefits; if a man shifts from full-time to a half-time job, he typically loses 80 percent of his income.[166] Most part-time jobs also offer little opportunity for promotion: About 25 percent of all college teachers now work part time, for example, but these adjunct professors get low pay and have no chance of getting tenure. Surveys of men have shown that 85 percent do not have any choice of work hours: They have either a full-time job or no job.[167]

You can get a part-time job if you want to be a sales clerk or flip hamburgers at a fast-food stand. But if you want to be an accountant, a factory worker, an engineer, a computer programmer, or a roofer, you have to apply for a standard 40-hour-a-week job. Despite the tremendous changes in the structure of the American family, we still have the same nine-to-five jobs that we have had ever since the 1930s.

The most important step toward giving workers more choice of their own schedules is to make discrimination against part-time workers illegal. The number of part-time workers has increased despite the disadvantages of most part-time jobs, and many more people would want to work part time if they could get decent pay and a chance at advancement. Part-timers should get the same hourly salary as full-time workers who do the same job and should get a pro-rated share of benefits. Part-timers should also have the same chance at promotion and the same job security as full-time workers if they have put in equivalent time on the job; there are some large corporations where the main disincentive to working shorter hours is a union contract that requires all part-time workers to be laid off before any full-time workers are laid off, and this sort of discrimination should be illegal.

First Steps

Because so many mothers of young children have entered the work force, a few businesses have begun to give them the option of working part time and other forms of job flexibility. Hewlett Packard was one of the first;

currently it has 450 employees taking advantage of job sharing as well as 5,000 telecommuters. First Tennessee Bank allows job sharing and gives benefits to part-time workers, as well as allowing telecommuting and flextime: When they decided to let full-time workers become part-timers without giving up their benefits, they found that 85 percent of the employees who were going to quit because of family obligations stayed on instead, saving on their training costs.[168] A spokesman for the U.S. Chamber of Commerce has endorsed giving employees with new children part-time work at pro-rated pay, because "there is very little out of pocket expense, and employees find it to be attractive."[169]

Businesses are just barely beginning to eliminate discrimination in promotions against part-time workers. For example, one of the country's most prestigious law firms now has a policy that women with children can cut back to half-time work for 3 years; if they do so, the time that they have to become partners in the firm will be extended from 7 to 11 years.[170] Similarly, one major university recently changed its rules to give all professors an extra year to get tenure if they have a child during that time. In an even larger step, one major brokerage firm now has three partners working part time.[171]

Part-time work has grown very rapidly, even with the discrimination in pay and promotion that many part-timers face. Flexible hours could become common if we passed laws that ban discrimination against part-time workers and offer tax incentives to corporations that offer part-time jobs. The government should also set an example by offering flexible hours wherever it is feasible.

The Netherlands is a model, since it has deliberately promoted part-time work to reduce unemployment. During the 1980s, when unemployment and inflation were rising, labor unions agreed to restrain their wage demands to fight inflation; in exchange, businesses agreed to provide more part-time jobs with comparable wages and benefits to fight unemployment by spreading the work around. Because of this compromise, called the Agreement of Wassenaar, the proportion of part-time workers increased from 21 percent in 1983 to 36.5 percent in 1996.[172]

Yet conventional feminists bristle at the idea of shorter hours, and particularly at part-time jobs, because they think it would turn women into second-rate employees. A number of years ago, Felice Schwartz wrote an article in the *Harvard Business Review* saying that corporations should recognize that there are two types of women employees: those who put their careers first, and those who are willing to sacrifice career advancement in order to have more flexible schedules and spend more time with their children. Feminists immediately labeled this second option the "mommy track," condemned it as a sort of second-class citizenship for women, and said that women could climb the corporate ladder just as ruthlessly and ignore their children just as thoroughly as any man.

One woman who is a partner in one of the country's largest law firms, specializing in mergers and acquisitions, said she found Schwartz's proposal "really offensive." But somehow her own life does not seem very satisfying, despite her six-figure income: "I drive around in a Volvo with a baby seat in the back and a car phone in front. If possible, I don't let myself focus on the frustrations. I just sort of bulldoze my way ahead."[173]

Anyone who has thought critically about the modern economy cannot help but wonder whether mergers and acquisitions are really as useful as the vital and real work of raising children. If people think that shorter work hours would make women second-class citizens, it is because they believe the useful work traditionally done by women is less important than the struggle for money and power, which was traditionally limited to men.

FAMILY-FRIENDLY TAX POLICIES

To let more families take care of their own children, we should also restore some of the family-friendly tax policies that the country adopted in the 1940s, which helped create the pro-family environment of the 1950s.

For example, in the late 1940s, Congress allowed a deduction of $600 for each dependent, equivalent to $6,500 in current dollars; but this deduction did not keep up with inflation and had lost most of its value by the 1990s. The child tax credit, beginning at $400 in 1998, was a step toward bringing it back to its original level, with the added benefit of converting it from a deduction, which is more valuable to families with higher tax rates, to a credit, which benefits all income levels equally. A larger credit—which should be refundable, so that low-income people could benefit fully from it—would help moderate-income families care for their children.

We should also eliminate the "marriage penalty" from the income tax code. In the late 1940s, Congress also allowed income splitting, which let married couples each pay tax on half their combined income, putting most married people in a lower tax bracket. But income splitting was eliminated in 1969, and tax reforms of the 1980s and 1990s put married couples at a disadvantage: Today, most married couples have to pay higher taxes than they would if they were both single. The simplest way to eliminate this penalty would be to restore income splitting.[174]

Finally, we need to make the tax code more progressive in order to reduce income inequality, which is now worse in the United States than in any other developed nation. Inequality is caused largely by global economic trends—the global economy has eliminated most of the well-paying factory jobs that unskilled American workers could get a few decades ago—but the tax system could mitigate it. Pretax child poverty rates are about the same in Britain, France, and the United States, but tax and transfer policies reduce child poverty to only 4 percent in France and 8 percent in Britain, compared with 20 percent in the United States.[175]

Our tax system became much less progressive in the 1980s, when the Reagan administration lowered and flattened income tax rates and increased the Social Security tax, which applies only to wages and salaries (not to income from investments) and exempts higher income above a certain threshold. People with higher incomes should pay their fair share of taxes, we should reduce taxes for moderate income people, and we should increase the earned income tax credit for low-income working people. The tax system should ensure that people who work do not have to live in poverty.

Although household incomes for most Americans have continued to go up during the past few decades, household incomes for lower-income Americans have actually declined in real terms. A fairer tax system would give working families with lower incomes a better chance of raising their own children.

NO-FAULT DIVORCE

Reform of no-fault divorce laws has probably been the most widely discussed of all the possible items of pro-family legislation.

Before the 1970s, most states allowed divorce only on the grounds of infidelity, desertion, or cruelty, and alimony settlements were used to punish the spouse who was at fault. The law also enforced sex-based roles after the divorce: Husbands were often required to support their ex-wives long after the divorce, and wives were almost always awarded custody of the children.

In 1970, California passed the nation's first no-fault divorce law, and virtually every other state had adopted no-fault divorce laws by 1985. Under these laws, either spouse can dissolve a marriage simply by saying that there are "irreconcilable differences." The spouse asking for a divorce does not have to prove fault, and the other spouse does not have to agree to the divorce. Property and alimony awards are based on need rather than on fault. In addition, old gender roles are discarded: Alimony is not expected to continue for life—only until the wife becomes self-supporting.

Recently, as we have learned how harmful divorce is to children, bills to reform no-fault divorce laws have been introduced in a number of state legislatures. Their backers point out that it is now easier to end a marriage than it is to break any other contract. Marriage is the only contract that one party can decide unilaterally to dissolve.

Centrists as well as conservatives have criticized no-fault divorce. For example, William Galston, a New Democrat and former Clinton adviser, has said that because the evidence shows divorce harms children unless the marriage involves abuse or extreme emotional cruelty, we should adopt a two-tier divorce system. Couples without dependent children should continue to use the current no-fault system, but couples with children should be required to wait a year even if both want the divorce and should be required to prove fault or to wait 5 years if only one wants the divorce.[176]

Opponents of divorce reform argue that no-fault divorce laws did not increase the divorce rate: Divorce rates were rising as sharply before these laws were passed as they did afterward. What they say is true, but they are overlooking an important function of the law.

Laws reflect and reinforce the moral sentiments of a community. During the technologically optimistic 1960s and 1970s, people believed in day-care centers, nursery schools, and other modern forms of child care, and the divorce rate went up because intact families no longer seemed necessary to raise children. States adopted no-fault divorce laws because people believed this, and these laws strengthened and legitimized this belief by giving it official government approval.

During the 1980s and 1990s, the divorce rate stabilized because people realized that strong families are essential. Reforming the divorce laws would also strengthen and legitimize this belief by giving it government approval.

But new divorce laws will help only if they make us take the family's functions more seriously. They will not help if we keep putting more and more children in infant preschool and in after-school programs, making the family less important in fact as it becomes more important in law.

5

HUMANIZING OUR ECONOMY

MONEY ECONOMY AND USE ECONOMY

Shorter, more flexible work hours are essential to let parents raise their own children, but the usual objection to shorter work hours is that people cannot afford them, because the typical family now needs two full-time incomes just to keep up with the bills.

According to one spokesperson for the National Association of Women (NOW), we need more day care because 94 percent of all families are so economically pressed that they cannot take care of their own preschool children: They cannot get along financially without two incomes, even for a few years.[177] This is an extreme claim, but it is a sign of the times.

This objection leads us straight to the central paradox of the modern economy. We feel harder pressed economically than people did in the past, even though we are much wealthier. In 1890, only one married women out of twenty worked for pay. Of the married women who did work, three-quarters were immigrants working in factories (usually in sweatshops) and most of the rest were Black women working as domestic servants.[178] Only the poorest of the poor felt that they needed a second income to get by. Today, after a century of economic growth, the average American has more than six times the income as in 1890 (after correcting for inflation),[179] but most American women feel that they absolutely must work out of economic necessity.

If there were flexible hours, most Americans would only reduce their work hours a bit if it meant lower income. In fact, labor unions oppose comp-time laws, which give workers the option of taking 1½ hours off for each hour of overtime they work rather than taking time-and-a-half pay, because they claim that workers not only need full-time jobs but also need overtime pay just to get by.

We have gotten into this bizarre situation by promoting growth of the money economy and devaluing the home and neighborhood economy, where people produce directly for use. The home economy still had vitality in the late nineteenth and early twentieth centuries, even though women's work was considered less important than men's. During the last few decades, we devalued the home economy even further as women entered the work force: We stepped up the rate of economic growth to bring women into the money economy along with men, and we let the home and neighborhood economy wither.

By the 1990s, parents spent 40 percent less time with their children than in 1965, largely because they had to spend the extra time at work.[180] We cannot expect the family to become stronger when more and more people are working full time, putting their children in day care, and eating fast food.

If we care seriously about our children, we have to think about changing the economy to make it work for families, rather than distorting family life to fit it into the economy. To restore the family, we need to bring more paid work into the home. Even more important, we need to consume less and work less in the money economy so that we can have more time for our unpaid work in the home economy.

In the last chapter, we looked at policies that deal directly with family issues, such as child-care allowances, school vouchers, and flexible work hours. But child-raising is only one responsibility of the home economy—which stands out because the home economy is just now losing it. Day care for infants and extended care for school children are just the final step in the long historical process of the money economy's undermining people's ability to do for themselves.

In this chapter, we will look at larger questions about economic growth and about creating a better balance between the money economy and the home and civil society. Child care is the one issue that is so emotionally charged that it could actually convince Americans that we would be better off if we consumed less and had more free time to do for ourselves.

WORKING AT HOME

At the turn of the twentieth century, it seemed inevitable that the economy would continue to become more centralized and that small-scale production at home would disappear, and feminists began to argue that women should and inevitably would get jobs: Women were simply "following their work out of the home."

But today's technology gives us much more economic choice than there was a century ago. The steam engine and other nineteenth-century technologies were only efficient when they were used on a large scale, but these technologies have long been obsolete. Electric power and computerization lend themselves either to centralization or to decentralization. Because today's technology is so flexible, we can make deliberate political decisions about whether to use it on a large scale or on a small scale.

Some changes that would bring work back into the home can be made rather easily, because they fit in with the way in which our technology is already evolving: Computers and telecommunications have already let more people work at home. Other changes require harder political and moral decisions. If we adopt policies to encourage these changes, both women and men will be able to follow their work back into the home.

The Electronic Cottage

What has been called "the electronic cottage" is already here and has been widely publicized. New technology makes it easier than ever before for people to do office work in their homes. Some futurists have predicted that this will lead to a reorganization of the relationship between home and work as significant as the one that occurred during the early Industrial Revolution, when work first began to move out of the home and into factories.

The American Home Business Association estimates that 27 million Americans work at home at least part time, and the chair of the association says that it is becoming more acceptable: "Working at home used to carry a stigma. It's grown and gained respect as computers and communications devices got smaller and cheaper."[181] Digital Equipment Company, DuPont, and US West (the regional telephone company based in Denver) began work-at-home programs during the 1980s, and many other businesses did the same in the 1990s. Likewise, the state of Colorado allows all its agencies to offer employees an option that it calls "flexplace," which lets them work at home, and some agencies of the federal government offer a similar program.

New technology makes it easy and affordable to set up a well-equipped home office. You can now get a computer with a fax/modem for as little as $1,000. High-quality personal copiers, which produce output as good as office copiers, are available for as little as $1,300. A telephone answering machine, which takes the place of a secretary, costs less than $100. These electronic devices are becoming less expensive, and a home office will become even more affordable in the future.

At today's prices, it is possible to put together a fully equipped, "state-of-the-art" home office for less than $5,000. Most people could save this much in commuting costs in a few years by working at home. If you count the full costs of commuting—including the environmental costs—savings in commuting costs alone could recover the cost of equipping a home office in less than 2 years, an extraordinarily high return on an investment.

New technology has made the electronic cottage possible, but changes in the family have made it popular. One survey found that two-thirds of the people who work at home are in two-income families, and more than half have children under 18 at home.[182] Doing at least part of one's work at home seems particularly appropriate for families with older children who are already in school. These children do not have to be supervised closely and do not demand so much attention that they make it impossible to work, but most parents do not want to have latchkey children who have to come home from school and let themselves into an empty house. In fact, studies have shown that just the presence of a parent in the house when children come home from school time reduces the risk of substance abuse, violence, and suicide.[183] Yet there are an estimated 5 million to 7 million latchkey children in the United States who are home alone after school; for example, one-third of all 12-year-olds stay home by themselves while their parents work.[184]

Some parents of very young children also manage to work at home. For example, Alice, a secretary in Portland, Oregon, thought at first that she could keep her job after having a child only if her husband worked the night shift at his assembly-line job, so that he could take care of the baby during the day. But the owner of the small engineering firm where she worked solved her family's problem by letting her stay home and still work as his personal secretary. He provided her with a computer, printer, copier, and a dedicated phone line connecting her with his office. She answers his calls and transfers them to him by pressing two buttons; callers do not know that she is at home, that he also has started working in an office in his own home, 10 miles away, and that she meets with him face to face only a couple of times a week, when she drives over to drop off documents. Her salary was lowered a bit, but she saved herself an hour and a half of commuting each day. She now has two toddlers as well as her job, and she says that her life is hectic but that she never would trade it for an ordinary office job.

There is a real need for tax incentives to encourage businesses to allow the sort of telecommuting that Alice does. Currently, about half of all home workers, about 13 million in all, run their own independent businesses. Many of these are well-paid consultants; because they have the most skills, they tend to be given the most freedom. About 3 million others have regular jobs and also work at small home businesses to supplement their incomes. About 10 million are able to take work home part time from a regular job. But only about 600,000 are allowed to hold regular jobs and to telecommute— that is, to work at home, as Alice does, with an electronic connection to their offices. We should give businesses tax breaks that encourage them to let more of their employees do at least part of their work at home, like the high-paid consultants.

Modern technology has opened up many new ways to work that never existed before, and it is up to us to decide which are best on social and political grounds. Two television advertisements, which ran at the same time a number of years ago, set out the alternatives very clearly.

One ad for United Airlines showed a young mother dropping her child off at a day-care center and then flying to a meeting in Chicago. The camera cuts back and forth between shots of the child playing happily and the mother sitting at the meeting and glancing furtively at her watch. After the meeting ends, she rushes to the airport, flies home, and picks up her child at the day-care center exactly on time—thanks to United Airlines.

Another advertisement, for Macintosh Computer, showed a pregnant woman describing her plan to be back at work 1 week after the baby is born. When a friend asks if she thinks she "can run a $10-million business from the nursery," she answers, "No, I think I can run it from the den"—by using her Macintosh computer.

Compare the environmental effects of these two visions of the immediate future: driving miles on the freeway to the child-care center and the airport and then flying thousands of miles to a meeting, versus staying at home with a computer that uses about as much energy as a single light bulb. The way of life the United Airlines ad sketches is exactly what we must avoid if we really care about leaving a livable world to our children and grandchildren.

Just as important, compare the moral and political effects of these two visions of the future. One mother works for someone else, has someone else raise her child, is constantly on someone else's schedule, and spends much of her time in the controlled, engineered world of freeways, airplanes, and airports; she is a Very Important Person, but she has very little say about running her own life or her child's life. The other mother works for herself, raises her own child, and makes her own schedule; she uses modern technology, rather than being controlled by it.

Production for Use

In addition to bringing paid work into the home, we need to revive the informal home economy, that is, family production for its own use.

Today's technology lets us choose among many different methods of production. For example, modern technology makes it possible for the money economy to take over food preparation almost totally. For the first time in history, people can keep a supply of frozen dinners in their freezers and pop one into the microwave oven when they are ready to eat. For the first time, you can live on mass-produced meals, with no forethought, planning, or skill needed on your part.

On the other hand, it is also easier than ever before for people to prepare their own food from scratch; for example, yogurt-making machines let you put in the milk and starter, turn on the electricity, and then just forget about it for a few days. Small machines are also available for other forms of home production: power tools for home carpentry, for example, and electronic sewing machines that let you program the stitch and do your embroidery automatically.

Small machines have already belied one common prediction about women's work moving out of the home. In the late nineteenth century, clothes washing was mechanized in large commercial laundries where rotary washers and centrifugal extractors were all attached to an overhead drive shaft powered by a steam engine. This hot, unpleasant factory work was less of a burden than the housewife's hand-work with washtubs, washboards, and flat irons, and progressives such as Edward Bellamy and Charlotte Perkins Gilman predicted that, in the twentieth century, all washing would be collectivized in public laundries. Today, of course, most American households have their own electric washers and dryers, and there are fabrics that do not need ironing: Doing the wash at home is not pleasant, but it is less unpleasant than working in a Victorian factory laundry.

During the twentieth century, much production did move from the home into the money economy because mass production was more efficient, but the money economy also took over in cases where home production was more efficient, because everyone believed in progress. During the 1920s and 1930s, Ralph Borsodi found that, by using the most efficient small machinery available, he could produce canned tomatoes (for example) for 20 to 30 percent less than the price of tomatoes canned at the factory of the Campbell Soup Company.[185] More recently, the economist Scott Burns found that by spending a few minutes using an electric yogurt-maker, a family can "earn" the equivalent of more than twice the average wage for a few minutes of factory work.[186]

In our affluent economy, though, these calculations of efficiency do not have to be the overriding consideration. Most people will grow their own vegetables only if they enjoy that sort of work, and they will buy the things that they do not enjoy making themselves. If they hate gardening, people will not grow and preserve their own vegetables to save 20 cents on the cost of a can of tomatoes. The gardening, baking, and other home production that people still choose to do is more like a do-it-yourself hobby than like the unavoidable daily work of subsistence farmers: Rather than the Victorian household drudge, the model is Martha Stewart.

Learning by Doing

For young children, home production is an invaluable way of learning educational basics. For example, following a recipe is a good introduction to numbers and counting for children. At the beginning, toddlers can watch their parent count out how many measures of flour or how many eggs are needed. Before long, they try to help by doing the counting as the parent scoops out the flour. Then they scoop out the flour themselves, and they can use the arithmetic they have learned at school to double or halve the size of a recipe.

For adolescents, home production is invaluable for developing a sense of competence and good habits. If you are making something, you learn that orderliness, patience, and diligence are not just character traits that adults lecture you about in order to make your life less pleasant; they are essential to getting anything done. Adolescents do not learn this working at McDonald's, where the business organizes the materials and tells them what motions to go through. And they do not learn this at home if the only productive work they do there is putting frozen dinners into the microwave oven.

If you put your children in a very expensive, very progressive preschool, where the teachers believe in learning by doing, you might be able to get them in a program that exposes them to this sort of small-scale production. But a school program is not as good as really making something at home. It is just an academic exercise in learning by doing: The child is not actually making something that is practical and necessary. Home production shows children that there is a direct relationship between effort and result, that you can get something you actually want or need by making it yourself.

Appropriate and Practical Technology

The "appropriate technology" movement, which was very popular during the 1970s, advocated this sort of small-scale production for use, but it was too romantic to have much of an effect. Plenty of books were sold that told the stories of people who went back to the land and lived solely on what they produced with their own labor, but though it is interesting to read about, most people are not going to raise a flock of chickens, put their manure into a compost digester, and use the methane gas that they collect to cook the eggs for breakfast.

The kinds of production for use that can have a real effect on our economy are much less romantic: They are the sorts of things that our parents or grandparents did as a matter of course, without mentioning the word "technology." It is practical to cook your own meals rather than getting take-out, to walk to the store rather than driving, and to take care of your own children rather than using day care. It is most important to do the things that the money economy cannot do adequately, such as raising children: Store-bought tomatoes are almost as good as tomatoes from your own garden, but store-bought day care does not compare with a child's own parents.

Ironically, most of the people who had romantic fantasies about going back to the land and being self-reliant ended up as dual-income couples when they got older, and now they do not have time to do even simple things for themselves. Their parents took it for granted that they should cook their own dinner, and some used to make the extra effort of making their own lunch and bringing it to work in a brown paper bag; but they go out for lunch and also get take-out for dinner, because they do not have time to cook. Their parents had one car, but they need two cars. Their parents took care of their own preschool children, but they use day care.

VOLUNTARY SIMPLICITY

People do not have the time for home production—not even for simple things like cooking or caring for their own children—because economic pressures make them feel they need two full-time incomes. Most Americans do not want a steady diet of fast food, any more than they want to put their babies in day care. But families today feel they need two incomes to get by, and they cannot spare the extra time or energy to do anything productive at home. To restore the balance between the money economy and the home economy, we need to cut back on consumerism to leave ourselves time for more important things.

More affluent Americans usually find that they can change their lives just by making different personal choices. There is a growing "voluntary simplicity" movement in America today. The best-selling book *Your Money or Your Life*[187] tells Americans how to consume less so they can have more time for themselves, and its authors say that frugality is penetrating mainstream culture: A few years ago, when they were on talk shows, 10 or 20 percent of the callers said that their ideas were totally impractical, but now no one is saying that any longer.[188]

There have been many articles in popular magazines about parents who made the transition from being a dual-income to being a single-income family so that they could take care of their own children. Most of these families reduce their spending on entertainment more than on anything else. For example, one couple gave up what they called the "budget-busting bistro suppers" that they had when they were a childless, two-paycheck couple and rented VCRs instead of going out to movies.[189] They began living on one income a year before their child was born and saved the second income during this time: Almost half the savings they accumulated during their 8-year marriage were from this single year.

Another couple went from two incomes to one when their children were 4 and 2 years old, after sitting down with a financial planner to set their goals and to see where their spending could be cut. The largest saving, as usual, was on entertainment, baby-sitting, and clothing, where they cut expenses by more than three-quarters. Another major saving was on day care, as might be expected, where they cut expenses by almost three-quarters. They also saved a considerable amount by cooking at home, cutting their food expenses by more than half. And they decided to avoid using charge accounts: "We used to buy what we wanted. Now I think about needs instead of wants."[190] As a result, they actually begin saving money for the first time when they shifted to one income; before, they had always lived from one paycheck to the next.

These articles show that affluent families can go from two incomes to one—and actually save more—simply by giving up gourmet restaurants, movies, impulsive credit-card spending, and the like. This sort of luxury spending is common among dual-income families, and the current child-care tax credit subsidizes it.

These articles are usually about changes that are conservative: from being the conventional dual-income family of the 1990s to being something more like a conventional suburban family of the 1950s. Yet there are things about them that are undeniably necessary if we are going to move toward a better society: less impulse buying, more home cooking, more time (and less money) spent taking care of your own children.

DRIVING TO THE POOR HOUSE

Wealthier families can make time to care for their own children by making personal choices to cut down on luxury spending, but for moderate-income families to make time, we have to make political choices. The largest single example of waste in the American economy is one that most families cannot choose to avoid: the high cost of transportation and housing in cities that have been rebuilt around the automobile.

During the last 50 years, the American city has been rebuilt as a sprawl of freeways, shopping malls, business parks, and housing tracts where people absolutely have to drive a car every time they leave their homes. Though planners in the 1960s were already saying that our cities were far too dependent on the automobile, the average American drives more than twice as much now as in 1970.[191] This is a burden to wealthier families but much more of a burden to low- and moderate-income families, whose budgets are stretched to the breaking point.

This sort of urban sprawl did not even exist when our parents or grandparents were born. Yet most people now have no choice but to pay for a suburban house and two cars, and they take this way of life totally for granted.

The Rise and Fall of the Suburbs

To get a clear idea of how wasteful the modern American economy is, we should look at our cities in historical context and see how radically they were rebuilt around new forms of transportation during the last two centuries.

Early in the nineteenth century, only the wealthy owned carriages, and walking was the usual form of transportation for most people who lived in cities, as it had been throughout history. Cities had always been built around the pedestrian, dense enough that people could get to any destination in the city by walking. Urban density had to be very high, typically about 100 people per acre, as it still is in the older parts of European cities, and people lived in apartments or in narrow row-houses.

During the nineteenth century, as steam-powered ferry boats and horse-drawn omnibuses became popular, the American middle class moved to new neighborhoods of three- to four-story row-houses that were set back a bit from the street and had private backyards. These row houses were built on lots of about one-twentieth of an acre, and their neighborhoods had overall densities of about 30 people per acre. Many of these neighborhoods have been revived in the past few decades, and they are still very livable.

Toward the end of the nineteenth century, cable cars and electric trolley cars were invented, and they let the middle class move to "streetcar suburbs" made up two- or three-story houses, with front porches, small front and side yards, and substantial backyards. These houses were generally built on lots of about one-tenth of an acre, and their neighborhoods had densities of 15 people per acre. Wealthy people lived on larger lots in more remote suburbs built around railroad stations, but middle-class Americans could not afford to pay train fare every day or to maintain a carriage to take them home from the train station, so they lived in streetcar suburbs, commuted by trolley, and walked home from the station.

The United States led the world in building streetcar lines before World War I, and this sort of neighborhood spread all over the country, in small towns as well as large cities. Now, we look back at it as the classic American neighborhood. People who lived in these neighborhoods did not own private vehicles: They used streetcars for commuting, and walking was their main form of transportation for other trips. Even though these neighborhoods were much less dense than traditional cities, everyone lived within walking distance of a local shopping street, where there were grocery stores, doctors' and dentists' offices, newsstands, clothing stores, and all the other stores you need on a day-to-day basis—as well as the streetcar line that took you to other parts of town.

There were also small corner stores right in the neighborhoods, and many corner grocery stores offered deliveries for people who did not want to carry groceries home. Stores that sold heavy furniture or appliances all delivered to your home.

People could sit out on the front porch and see their neighbors walk by. People knew their neighbors not only in small towns but even in the largest cities: one person who grew up in this sort of neighborhood in Brooklyn during the 1920s remembers that, within a few weeks after they moved in, her mother knew all 34 families on their block.

Unfortunately, these streetcar suburbs were built for only a few decades. The automobile became popular not long after the electric trolley, and by the 1920s the middle class was beginning to move to neighborhoods of bungalows on one-sixth-acre lots, where it was a bit difficult to get around by walking. As George Babbitt said in Sinclair Lewis's 1922 novel, "It's the fellow with . . . an automobile and a nice little family in a bungalow on the edge of town, that makes the wheels of progress go round."[192]

After World War II, the federal government greased the wheels of progress by building freeways, and the middle class moved to modern suburbs where it is impossible to walk. Houses are on quarter-acre lots on cul-de-sacs, and stores are in shopping centers surrounded by acres of parking, so you cannot go to buy a newspaper or a cup of coffee without driving your car. Modern suburbia has overall densities as low as 2 people per acre, much lower than the 15 per acre in Victorian suburbs. Half to two-thirds of the land in a typical American city is used to accommodate the automobile,[193] and the automobile uses even more land indirectly, because people want to live in low-density housing to avoid noise, to reduce the danger to children, and to keep traffic congestion down to a bearable level.

From the walking city, to row-house neighborhoods, to streetcar suburbs, neighborhoods became more livable. But when we compare the streetcar suburbs with modern suburbia, our neighborhoods seem to have become less livable. Residential streets are noisier and more congested. Air and water quality are worse. Neighborhoods are less safe: Automobile accidents are the number-one cause of death among children. People are less likely to know their neighbors. And the parking lots and commercial strips are just plain ugly. Despite all the extra money we spend to live in suburbia, the quality of life has deteriorated.

The complex of suburbs and automobiles places a tremendous financial burden on Americans. The automobile absorbs about 20 percent of the average family's disposable income directly; and it also has many hidden costs, such as the cost of "free" parking at shopping centers (which is added to the price of goods and services) and the extra costs of air pollution. Housing absorbs about 30 percent of the typical family's income: The size of the typical house has more than doubled since 1950,[194] and sprawl has also driven up housing prices by driving up the price of land.

Between them, housing and transportation absorb about 50 percent of Americans' disposable income, making life hard for the middle class and almost intolerable for the working class.

Lavinia and William Johnson both grew up in a working-class neighborhood in Cleveland, where their grandparents and their parents' extended families also lived, and their fathers both worked at blue-collar factory jobs during the 1950s and 1960s. But most of the factories closed in the 1970s, so William works as a checker at a supermarket and Lavinia works as a receptionist. William does not earn as much as his father did; after correcting for inflation, his wages are more like what his grandfather used to earn. But his expenses are much higher: During the 1970s, when they had children, he and his wife moved to an older suburb outside the city limits.

The middle class left Cleveland in the 1950s and 1960s, and the working class left in the 1970s and 1980s. In all, Cleveland's population dropped from over 900,000 in 1950 to just over 500,000 in 1990, while the population of the surrounding suburban counties increased by about the same amount. Like most people who left after 1970, the Johnsons felt they had no choice. Crime was increasing. Their old block no longer felt like a family neighborhood and was beginning to look bombed out. Most important, they did not want their children in the inner-city public schools, and the only way they could get into a better school system was by moving to the suburbs. In the old neighborhood, their grandparents took the bus to work and walked to do their shopping, but they both need to drive to work.

Lavinia's grandmothers and mother stayed home until the children started school, but between the lower wages and the higher expenses, she had to work full time just to make ends meet. She and William considered themselves lucky that they got their children into day-care and Head Start programs funded by the federal government. Now that their children are grown up and working at low-wage service jobs in an age when government is cutting spending, they are having much more trouble finding affordable day care for their own children.

Their neighborhood was built as a working-class suburb right after World War II, and it looks like lower-cost postwar suburbs all over the country. There are endless rows of nondescript one-story houses, each with a patch of front lawn on one side and a wide driveway filled with two or three cars on the other side. And there are the endless shopping strips lined with the same fast-food stands and gas stations—where every business has its own parking lot, where the traffic is brutal, and where you never see anyone walking. Working-class families have to put their children in day care and earn two incomes in order to pay for *this*.

Building Neighborhoods

Talk about streetcar suburbs is not just nostalgia. The most important trend in urban planning today is called the "New Urbanism" or "Traditional Neighborhood Design."[195] Peter Calthorpe, Andres Duany and Elizabeth Plater-Zyberk, and many other urban designers, have begun to build new neighborhoods modeled on the streetcar suburbs built before World War I. To encourage a sense of community, these neighborhoods are designed with smaller lots than modern suburbia, so that people can walk to local shopping and to transit stops, and the houses have front porches.

When Duany first built this sort of neighborhood in Seaside, Florida, many realtors predicted it would fail: They asked why people should buy a house on a small lot when the same money could get them a house on a quarter-acre of land in a conventional suburb. But Seaside was tremendously successful because people like to live in a community where they can sit on their front porches and see neighbors whom they know walking by, and similar projects are being built all over the country. *Emerging Trends in Real Estate*, the nation's most respected real estate forecast, has said that the New Urbanism is the most important trend in real estate development today.[196] In what must be the ultimate mark of respectability, Disney Corporation has endorsed the New Urbanism, by building the town of Celebration, Florida, in this style.

This movement has influenced regional planning as well as neighborhood design. The master plan of Portland, Oregon, which began with a study by the well-known New Urbanist Peter Calthorpe, includes an urban growth boundary to prevent sprawl, new light-rail service, and zoning to concentrate new neighborhoods within walking distance of transit stops. Most urban planners consider Portland the most important national model for the future; even the *Wall Street Journal*, not usually known for being antigrowth, has said that Portland's planning has made it an "Urban Mecca,"[197] so livable that planners from all over the country are coming to study it.

Houses in New Urbanist style are estimated to cost 30 percent less to build than conventional suburban houses with the same square footage—because of savings on land and on site infrastructure such as roads and utility lines.[198] There are also big savings on transportation. Peter Calthorpe points out that people in suburbs built early in the twentieth century drive about half as much as people who live in newer sprawl suburbs, saving the average family about $9,000 a year in travel costs.[199] At one of his developments, a bank set up a special mortgage plan that let people qualify for loans with lower incomes than they would require in a conventional development; the bank recognized that the full cost of buying a home is not only the cost of the house itself but also the cost of the transportation you need to live there. Environmentalists have suggested that all banks should offer this sort of "location-efficient mortgage" for houses in pedestrian-oriented neighborhoods, and the federal government has started a pilot program to fund them.[200]

During the 1950s, there were many books of popular social criticism about the new suburbs that were sprouting up all over the country—books with names like The *Split-Level Trap* and *The Crack in the Picture Window*—all of them arguing that even the well-to-do families that moved to the suburbs were heavily burdened by the cost of the mortgage and the cost of maintaining a second car. The husband had a long commute to work, which left him with less time for his family. His job was not satisfying: He was much less likely than his grandfather or even his father to be working at his own business, and much more likely to be an "organization man" working for a big corporation. He came home tired and drank two martinis while his wife got the children ready for bed. The irony was that he moved to suburbia for the sake of his family, but the suburban way of life left him no time for his family.

Today, the irony is much more bitter. More Americans now live in the suburbs than in the city or the country; most households own two or more cars; and, in most families, both spouses have to work to support this way of life. The suburban husband of the 1950s could not spend as much time with his family as he wanted, but he could at least comfort himself with the thought that his children were well taken care of at home. Today's parents do not even have this consolation.

THE NEIGHBORHOOD ECONOMY

Old-fashioned neighborhoods had social networks that let them perform important productive functions, but American neighborhoods lost this sense of community after World War II. For example, one study of a 1950s suburb showed that people who lived there could identify only the five neighboring families who lived in the houses next to theirs and directly across the street.[201] These are the neighbors they could see out of their own windows; they never walked down the block and saw the other neighbors. In 1950s suburbs, the front porch was replaced by a patio or deck in the back, since no one wants to sit in front of the house and watch cars roll by.

The neighborhood lost its productive functions because modern suburbia isolates families, but we could revive the neighborhood economy if we built traditional neighborhoods and if people had free time.

Children in the Neighborhood

The neighborhood used to give the home invaluable help with child care. Parents in modern suburbia send children to preschools and organized play groups because there are no children around for them to play with. But in the streetcar suburbs, where there were dozens of families on the block and you knew them all, there were children to play with right there.

Somehow, these children managed to make do very well without "state-of-the-art" facilities. An old clothes line was all you needed for a game of jump rope, with jumping rhymes that were handed down unchanged even after they were obviously out of date: In the 1970s, girls were still chanting rhymes about Charlie Chaplin; but this minor genre of folk culture has almost disappeared now that most children play games organized by adults.

Neighborhoods taught children lessons that they do not learn in schools. When they wanted to play ball, they chose up teams and umpired the games for themselves, rather than being organized by adults into Little League teams. When they wanted company, they could play with the other children on the block; when they wanted solitude, they could play alone in their backyards. Some parents were always nearby, keeping half an eye on them to make sure there was no trouble, but the parents did not organize their play. The most important thing the children learned was to use their own time and to organize themselves according to their own rules, rather than being scheduled and organized in groups by others.

We still use a few phrases that refer to the gang of neighborhood children who played together—we say that someone "is the new kid on the block" or "thinks he is the toughest kid on the block"—even though most Americans today do not have a group of kids on the block at all. People think it is absolutely necessary to put children in day care, summer camp, and Little League because they will not be "socialized" if they stay at home, where there are no other children for them to play with. If we began to build old-fashioned neighborhoods again, and if we had more parents and children who stayed at home, the neighborhood could take back its old role in child care.

Neighborhoods also used to have local handymen, baby-sitters, gardeners, and the like. Even more important, women had informal barter systems with kinfolk, neighbors, and friends, who helped each other care for children and the sick and do other domestic work.[202] As men entered the money economy, women preserved the older tradition of local barter and neighborly help, which had been essential when families worked on homesteads and needed each other's help in productive activities that ranged from harvesting to barn raisings. This helped preserve the mutual trust that had existed in traditional communities but that seems to be disappearing today, as professionals take over all the work.

Today, some activists are trying to create neighborhood barter networks to revive this sort of informal local economy. In a few places, such as Ithaca, New York, activists have even created local "currencies," which are used to help people trade services.[203]

Civil Society

Women preserved another vital feature of the traditional economy as men were absorbed by the money economy: the local voluntary organizations that we now call "civil society." During the nineteenth and early twentieth centuries, women volunteers helped to organize and run hospitals, playgrounds, libraries, museums, and concert halls. Women also played a central role in all of the political reform movements of the time, from the abolitionist, feminist, and temperance movements of the nineteenth century to the movements to abolish child labor, rebuild the slums, and establish juvenile courts in the early twentieth century. During the 1920s, as Victorian idealism was going out of fashion, one critic complained that club women in the Midwest used their talk about moral and civic improvement to exercise tyrannical power over the arts and politics, and that women in the East and West were not far behind.[204]

Recently, studies by Robert Putnam and other social scientists have focused everyone's attention on the decline of civil society in America today. Putnam has shown that membership in groups such as the PTA, the League of Women Voters, the Elks Club, and the Red Cross has declined by 25 to 50 percent over the last few decades, and the time people spend on voluntary organizations has declined by about 50 percent. In addition, the time people spend on informal socializing and visiting has declined by about 25 percent. People are less likely to go to political meetings, and they are also less likely to join bowling leagues.[205]

In trying to correlate the decline of civic participation with other social changes, Putnam concluded that its cause was the extra time that people spend watching television, but watching television is actually a *symptom* of the decline of civic life rather than its *cause*. People watch television when they have nothing better to do; they do not avoid other activities because they are so excited by the television that they cannot drag themselves away from it to do something else.

Civic participation declined because postwar America devalued the home and neighborhood and put its faith in the money economy. Even in the 1920s, women volunteers were becoming less important: Although they still joined groups in large numbers, the professional staffs of these groups were more likely to make the important decisions. The adults who moved to the suburbs in the 1950s still remembered the older values they had grown up with, and they joined the PTA and other local organizations, even though volunteers had little real power. And, as Putnam says, participation declined dramatically among the first generation that grew up in the postwar suburbs and learned that the money economy does all the serious work.

The decline of civil society parallels the decline of the family. The people who moved to the postwar suburbs tried to revive the family, but suburban housewives were discontented and restless living in homes that no longer had any important productive function, and the family revival collapsed in the 1960s and the 1970s when the children who grew up in these suburbs came of age. Likewise, the people who moved to the postwar suburbs joined PTAs and clubs and other civic organizations, but these volunteer groups no longer had an important productive function, and civic participation collapsed when the people who grew up in these suburbs came of age.

Today, both women and men expect to get more of their satisfaction from the money economy and less from home and community than Americans did in the past. If Americans had a more balanced view of what is important in life, we would want to live in real neighborhoods rather than bedroom suburbs, we would want to be active in our communities, and we would want to spend more time with our families. Both women and men would take more time for the neighborhood and home economy.

THE POLITICS OF FREE TIME

There is nothing sacred about the 40-hour week. The Roosevelt administration happened to settle on 40 hours as a compromise—and, in fact, it almost adopted a 30-hour week. And there is no reason to keep the 40-hour week in the face of the vast changes in the American family and the American economy since we adopted it in the 1930s.

During the first century of industrialization, the work week became shorter as production became more efficient: As wages went up, workers took advantage of part of the wage increase to improve their standard of living and part of the wage increase to give themselves more free time. Work time was cut in half between the 1830s and the 1930s. After World War II, though, during the prosperous postwar decades, the workweek stopped getting shorter. And during recent decades, work hours have actually gotten longer.

More Money or More Time

A few decades ago, everyone believed that better technology would give us both higher incomes and more free time. What happened to stop this?

Traditionally, farmers worked about 12 hours per day, and during the early nineteenth century, most industrial workers also had to work 12 hours a day, 6 days a week. By the mid-nineteenth century, however, wages were rising and the average workweek was falling slowly but steadily. By 1909, the workweek had gone down to 50 hours. During the 1920s, the 6-day, 48-hour week became standard. Finally, in 1931–1932, the 5-day, 40-hour week became standard.[206]

At the time, many economists thought we would eventually reach a point where people's material needs were satisfied, and workers would take advantage of further wage increases purely by reducing their hours. John Maynard Keynes was stating a common opinion when he wrote that, because of improved technology, "a point may soon be reached . . . when these [economic] needs are satisfied in the sense that we prefer to devote our further energies to non-economic purposes."[207] Then, he predicted, "man will be faced with his real, his permanent problem—how to occupy the leisure which science and compound interest have won for him, to live wisely and agreeably and well."[208]

Although most people do not remember it today, there was a political battle during the 1920s and early 1930s over whether America should take advantage of new technology by shortening work hours or by consuming more.[209]

Before the 1920s, labor unions argued that shorter hours would reduce fatigue and improve the efficiency of workers, and business generally accepted this argument. There is evidence that workers actually wanted the shorter hours so that they could have more time for their families, friends, and communities, but unions talked about efficiency to present their demands in a way that appealed to businessmen's values. After the unions won an 8-hour day during the 1920s and began demanding a 5-day, 40-hour week, they could not justify an entire extra day off by saying that giving workers more rest between shifts would increase efficiency. Unions began talking about the positive benefits of extra leisure, and employers resisted this challenge to business values.

During the 1920s, economists began to talk about "demand saturation"—people were beginning to feel they had enough and resisted buying more—and businessmen began to advocate what they called a "new gospel of consumption" to keep the economy growing and create more work. This was a common opinion during that decade: One newspaper editorial of the 1920s proclaimed that "the way to make business boom is to buy," and another editorial claimed that "the American citizen's first importance is no longer that of citizen but that of consumer. Consumption is the new necessity."[210]

When the Depression came, labor unions—led by William Green, president of the AFL—challenged these business values by calling for a shorter workweek rather than more consumption. They argued that shorter hours would let us avoid unemployment by sharing necessary work, rather than by creating unnecessary work. Shorter hours would also give workers more time for their families, for cultural activities, and for do-it-yourself projects, which would give them the satisfaction that work no longer provided now that factory production had replaced crafts production.

To deal with the unemployment caused by the Depression, labor supported the Black–Connery bill, which would have reduced the workweek to 30 hours. At the time, virtually everyone believed that the 30-hour week would just be the first step and that work hours would inevitably become even shorter in the future, as technology continued to become more efficient. Experimental work-sharing programs during the Depression seemed to be successful. After Kellogg's started a 30-hour workweek at its factory in Battle Creek, Michigan, a survey of workers showed that they enjoyed the extra free time, which they spent with their families, in community activities such as amateur sports, clubs, and churches, and in adult education courses.[211]

Initially, the Roosevelt administration supported the Black–Connery bill, and it passed the Senate in 1933, but business resisted it fiercely, arguing that we needed to fight unemployment by promoting more consumption rather than by shortening work hours. Because of business opposition, the administration changed its position; as a compromise, it backed the Fair Labor Standards Act, which reduced the workweek to 40 hours—not really a reduction for most workers, since the average workweek had already gone down to 33 hours because of the Depression—and it also promised more funding for public works projects to stimulate the economy and to provide everyone with a full-time 40-hour job.

During the postwar period, this compromise became the conventional wisdom: Everyone agreed that we needed to promote economic growth in order to create more 40-hour jobs. Businesses stepped up their advertising. The federal government stimulated the economy by using deficit spending, by building freeways, and by insuring the mortgages on suburban housing. We can see the spirit of the time in a famous interview with President Eisenhower that occurred during the minor recession of 1958: When a reporter asked him what Americans could do to help the economy, he answered with one word: "Buy," and when the reporter asked him what people should buy, he answered: "Anything."[212]

These efforts to stimulate consumer demand succeeded in their goal of providing everyone with a 40-hour job—that is, they succeeded in stopping the historical trend toward shorter work hours. The average workweek remained about 40 hours from 1945 through the mid-1960s. There was no reduction of work hours at all during this period of widespread prosperity and economic growth.

The cost of keeping up with the rising standard of living has become more burdensome since the 1970s. Overall, Juliet Schor has estimated, the number of hours that the average American works has increased by more than 10 percent since 1969.[213] During the 1970s, women entered the work force en masse, and during the 1980s and 1990s, the average worker's hours went up by almost 4 percent, giving the United States the longest workweek in the world.[214]

Families feel they need two incomes to keep up with their expenses. Yet the statistics show that, despite economic stagnation, average income kept growing as more adults entered the work force: The amount that the average American spends on personal consumption has increased by more than 45 percent (after correcting for inflation) since our economy began to stagnate in 1973.[215] Inequality has increased, squeezing low-income families, but middle-income women have not gone to work to maintain their standard of living: They have gone to work to keep the standard of living growing.

In western Europe, because of high unemployment, many governments have begun to promote shorter work hours again. As we have seen, the Netherlands has done the most to promote part-time work since the Agreement of Wassenaar. Rudd Lubbers, the prime minister when these policies were implemented, has written:

> the Dutch are not aiming to maximize gross national product per capita. Rather, we are seeking to attain a high quality of life. . . . Thus, while the Dutch economy is very efficient per working hour, the number of working hours per citizen is rather limited. . . . We like it that way. Needless to say, there is more room for all those important aspects of our lives that are not part of our jobs, for which we are not paid and for which there is never enough time.[216]

Because of these policies, the Netherlands now has only 4 percent unemployment, the lowest in Europe, and an average workweek of only 31.7 hours.[217]

Impoverishing Wealth

During the 1950s, the federal government had to stimulate demand because we had reached a point where growth was unnecessary and people had to be convinced that they wanted more products. Today, we have reached the point where growth is destructive and is crowding out families, communities, and the environment. The central political issue of our time is whether we can tame economic growth before it undermines the natural and social systems that are the basis of any sustainable economy.

The statistics on national income show that the average American is twice as wealthy now as in 1960 and more than four times as wealthy as in 1920,[218] but we actually feel more economically pressed in many important ways than people did in 1960 or even in 1920. Today, we have more major appliances than people did earlier in the century, more automobiles, more freeways, more parking lots, more boutiques, and more gourmet restaurants. But we have less time; we worry about the declining sense of community and looming ecological crisis; we cannot even afford to take care of our own children.

Several studies have tried to document the failure of growth by subtracting the environmental and social costs of growth from the gross domestic product (GDP).[219] The most comprehensive of these studies, the Genuine Progress Indicator, shows that America's per-capita GDP has risen fairly steadily during the last 50 years, but that our actual well-being rose from 1950 until the late 1960s, leveled off during the 1970s, and then began to decline, and that we have now reached the point where Americans are actually less well off than we were in the late 1950s, though we are much richer.[220]

The issue of child care, more than any other, can make the average person think critically about economic growth and realize that our affluence makes us feel more impoverished than ever. When child-care advocates say that we need more funding for day care because 94 percent of all families cannot get along without a second income, we should remember that America started talking about demand saturation and the need for a new gospel of consumption back in the 1920s, when incomes were one-fourth what they are today, when walking was our most common form of transportation, and when nobody had ever heard the phrase "shop 'til you drop." Americans will begin to ask hard questions about our standard of living if they start to wonder why most of us cannot spare the time to take care of our own children today, as even poor people did in 1960 and in 1920.

6

A NEW DIRECTION

THE FALL AND RISE OF LIBERALISM

Liberals have lost much of their influence because they have become disillusioned with modernism but have not developed a new vision of the future to replace it. Nineteenth-century socialists idealized industrial mass society, and twentieth-century liberals went along with this ideal. A century ago—even 50 years ago—people were attracted by the modernist vision of a future where people work at mass-production jobs, live in mass-produced housing, and put their children in massive school and day-care systems. Today, people no longer want this sort of faceless mass society, but liberals still stick with the old modernist ideas they inherited from socialism: They genuinely want to help people, but the only way they can imagine doing it is by setting up centralized bureaucracies.

To break out of this box, liberals need new policies that help people do more for themselves, policies that support the family and civil society rather than replacing them with massive bureaucracies. This book's proposals—such as a larger tax credit for child care that could be used either to pay for day care or to help parents stay home with their own preschool children—are examples of the new direction that we need.

In many ways, this new direction recalls the Jeffersonian roots of American liberalism, which resisted economic growth as a threat to our self-reliance. American liberals did not become modernists until the twentieth century, and the modernist ideal is now dying. Ecological problems have made us see that modernization and growth are a threat to the natural environment, but liberals have not yet seen that modernization and growth are also a threat to the social environment, because they undermine the family and civil society.

Because liberals continue to demand more bureaucratic social services, as modernists have all through the last century, "family-values" conservatives have benefited politically from the public's uneasiness about the social effects of modernization. But conservatives refuse to see the real problem: that economic growth leaves us with less time to do for ourselves. For example, Ronald Reagan once praised women who stay home with their children by saying, "Unlike Sweden, . . . the mothers of America have managed to avoid becoming just so many more cogs in the wheels of commerce"[221]; though he did not realize it, this statement implies that American men *are* just cogs in the wheels of commerce—probably the strongest criticism of the modern economy that any American president has made since the days of Jefferson. Yet at the same time that he said mothers should stay home, Reagan boasted that his economic policies had created enough jobs to give America the highest "employment ratio" of any country in the world; apparently, he did not know that a higher employment ratio means more women working.

Conservatives constantly founder on this sort of self-contradiction, and liberals could dominate the political debate if they turned decisively in a new direction. We need to reject the old left's blind faith in progress, which makes it demand federally funded day care and other social services provided by centralized bureaucracies, and we need to move in just the opposite direction: working to preserve the family and other small-scale voluntary groups by limiting modernization. The success of the New Urbanism and the widespread interest in reviving civil society show that there is broad support for restoring a better balance between the formal economy and the informal work of home, neighborhood, and voluntary groups.

This new direction will also change feminist thinking—and we need to remember that modernism is just one historical stage feminism has gone through. As we have seen, when the Industrial Revolution first moved men's work out of the home in the 1830s and 1840s, Catharine Beecher and other feminists tried to increase women's power by insisting that men should control the business world and women should control the home, and most Victorian feminists wanted to spread the higher ideals of the home, to make the public world more homelike. Feminists turned to modernism only around the turn of the twentieth century, when progressives believed that the technological economy would displace the home economy entirely, and feminists such as Charlotte Perkins Gilman rejected women's traditional work as a throwback to more primitive times.

Mainstream feminists are still modernists: They look down on the home economy and want women working at full-time jobs, like men. But the old-left vision that triumphant modernization would lead us to an efficient, centrally planned industrial future, which had so much influence during the twentieth century, has lost its appeal—and so has the idea that we should all work full time and put our children in day care. Some ecologically oriented feminists have begun to move in a new direction, by saying that we should not deprecate the work traditionally done at home by women, such as raising children.

If we want to find a new direction for liberalism, we should begin with child care. This is the issue where liberals are still most committed to having centralized bureaucracies take over. And it is the issue where liberals could appeal most dramatically to ordinary Americans by supporting programs that help people do more for themselves.

THE ORGANIZATION PERSON

During the 1960s and 1970s, as American families were becoming more and more integrated into the money economy—as more children were being put into the day-care system, as more adults were getting nine-to-five jobs, and as more families were buying second cars for their dual commute—"radical" feminists were cheering them on and saying that this was the way to liberation.

Never in history has there been a radical movement for social change that succeeded with as little resistance from the powers that be as the women's movement of the 1960s and 1970s. In 1963, Betty Friedan wrote that women were stultified because the "feminine mystique" forced them to stay out of the work force and devote themselves totally to their homes and families. Within a few decades, most women—including most mothers of preschool children—were in the work force. We passed laws banning discrimination against women, and we even changed the language to remove any hint of discrimination, so that now we have police officers instead of policemen, firefighters instead of firemen, and Worker's Compensation instead of Workman's Compensation. As this unprecedented social change occurred, business leaders did not call out Pinkerton guards to suppress it, and they did not even denounce it as a threat to America's economic system.

Success that comes so quickly should make us question whether the modern women's movement was radical at all. In reality, this movement fit right into the corporate-state economy. Because it succeeded, all the adult population is expected to work in the economy, instead of just half. Because of the modern women's movement, we have moved from the 1950s organization man to today's organization person.

Mainstream organizations, such as the National Organization for Women (NOW), were so successful because they let themselves be co-opted by our usual style of politics: They tried to get a "bigger piece of the pie" for their constituents. Just as business groups lobby for higher profits, labor unions lobby for higher wages, and the elderly lobby for higher Social Security benefits, mainstream women's groups lobby for higher wages for women, more money for day care, and so on.

Apart from the merits of any of these demands, it should be obvious that this style of politics cannot pose a real challenge to the modern economy. It takes the technological economy for granted, and it just demands that the economy provide more money and more services for your self-interest group. Interest groups demanding a bigger piece of the pie cannot ask whether the pie itself is becoming less nourishing.

THE FAILURE OF THE LEFT

Apart from the consumerism of mainstream feminists, though, there is a deeper flaw in the ideology of many radical feminists. Their attacks on the "traditional family" were part of a modernist vision of the future that goes back to nineteenth-century socialism. Looking at the history of 1960s and 1970s radicalism can help us to understand the declining influence of the left during the past few decades and to clear away some of the dead wood that is in the way of a new vision of the future.

Socialists Against the Family

Socialism was the first important political movement to argue that modernization would inevitably destroy the family, which would become obsolete as its functions were taken over by a centralized mass economy. Friederich Engels wrote the book that was the most important socialist analysis of the issue, *The Origin of the Family, Private Property and the State*, published in 1884.

Engels wrote that the patriarchal family was the product of one phase of human cultural evolution: Economic changes had made it appear and coming economic changes would make it disappear. He believed that studies of classical myths and primitive societies proved that families in pre-classical Greece were matrilineal, that they had cooperative, egalitarian values, and that they had an easily dissolved form of marriage, which he called the "pairing marriage." This ideal form of marriage and family disappeared when the rise of private property brought patriarchy and strict monogamy. Among primitive people, personal possessions were so scanty that they could be distributed without any fuss when their owner died. But after animals were domesticated, men wanted to pass on their herds to their sons—so they wanted their wives to belong exclusively to them for life to be sure that they were giving their property to their own sons.[222] Patriarchal society depended on the sexual subordination of women to insure the line of inheritance from father to son.[223]

But today, Engels wrote over a century ago, we are "approaching a social revolution in which the hitherto existing economic foundations of monogamy will disappear."[224] Monogamy arose because men wanted to hand productive property down to their sons, but private ownership of the means of production was no longer appropriate in the era of large-scale modern industry. When the inevitable socialist revolution collectivizes the means of production, it will cause sweeping changes in the family.[225]

Marriage will be a matter of free choice, based on what Engels calls "sex love," and will dissolve as soon as sex love passes.[226] This new sort of marriage will become possible because the family will no longer have any practical function. With socialism, Engels says, "[p]rivate housekeeping is transformed into a social industry. The care and education of the children becomes a public matter."[227] There is no need for families to stay together, because the family no longer has any important role in the economy or in raising children.

Therapists Against the Family

During the twentieth century, social critics added a psychological dimension to Engels's attack on the family. Marxists said patriarchy was a form of political oppression. Freudians added that patriarchal authority was internalized to form the superego, and the post-Freudian left wanted to remove this psychological oppression also.

Freud believed that repression and neurosis were based on the Oedipus complex, which made infants internalize their father's authority, and he believed that the Oedipus complex was universal, because people must repress some of their impulses for any society to survive. His theory seemed to imply that the patriarchal family is universal, that the authoritarian father is a necessary part of human psychology.

During the 1920s, anthropologists disproved this idea of Freud's. Bronislaw Malinowski found that the Trobriand Islanders, in the South Pacific, had no idea of biological fatherhood. Malinowski could not convince them that men had anything to do with making babies: They considered this another silly story, like the stories that the missionaries tried to spread. Their society was matrilineal, and even the idea of the father did not exist.[228] Though Malinowski himself was rather conservative, sexual reformers used his "refutation of Freud" to prove that patriarchy, repression, and neurosis were not universal.

The most important reformer was Margaret Mead, whose 1928 book *Coming of Age in Samoa* is by far the most influential book of anthropology ever written. Mead was looking for ways to avoid the stormy adolescence common in Western cultures, and she argued that there is an almost total "absence of psychological maladjustment"[229] among Samoan adolescents because of their sexual freedom and their lack of bonding to their parents.

Mead claimed Samoans were well adjusted because they had a period of "free and easy experimentation"[230] with sex before marriage, and they did not take adultery very seriously after marriage, except among those of high rank.[231] As a result, they considered sex "a delightful experience, expertly engaged in. . . . The Samoans condone light love-affairs, but repudiate acts of passionate choice."[232]

Mead also argued that Samoans were well adjusted because their parents had very little say in raising them. They had extended families of 15 or 20 people, and children who had conflicts with their parents simply moved to the hut of a relative, without anyone making a fuss about it.[233] Older children were responsible for most of the day-to-day care of Samoan infants, and there was very little discipline before the age of 6 and no attempt to make infants feel guilty when they misbehave.[234]

Mead admitted that she had some doubts about the Samoans' character. She said that they were incapable of strong feelings or commitments, and because they were raised by the other children, they conformed to the standard of the peer group rather than developing individualized personalities.[235] Nevertheless, she concluded:

> However much we may . . . feel that important personalities and great art are not born in so shallow a society, we must recognize that here is a strong factor in the painless development from childhood to womanhood. For where no one feels very strongly, the adolescent will not be tortured by poignant situations.[236]

And she spent her career arguing that we Americans could learn from the Samoan family how to eliminate "the complexes, the bad conditionings of early childhood."[237]

Today, we know that Mead's description of Samoa was grotesquely inaccurate. Samoan families fiercely protect the virginity of their unmarried daughters. Parents believe they must beat young children to discipline them, and they forbid children to cry while they are being beaten. Children are strongly attached to their parents and are not allowed to move out of their homes. Samoa has a higher rate of juvenile delinquency and rape than the United States.[238]

Mead never lived with a Samoan family; she got her data from interviews with 25 adolescent girls. Samoans often tell lies to people to dupe or tease them:[239] It seems likely that Samoan girls, who generally are ashamed to talk about sex, reacted to this stranger who kept asking them intimate questions by duping her in this way, making up silly stories about casual premarital promiscuity.

Yet Mead found exactly what she was looking for in Samoa, and her book was tremendously popular because it told its readers what they wanted to hear about sexual and family reform—that we could do away with maladjustment and neurosis by eliminating the guilt and repression caused by strong families.

The 1960s and the 1970s

Sixties radicals synthesized Marx and Freud. For example, Erich Fromm believed, like Engels, that the rise of private property and patriarchy were the source of all political oppression—and he added that patriarchy was the source of all Oedipal conflicts and neurosis. Fromm said the patriarchal family would disappear when modernization brought about a collective economy—and he added that the socialist society must be planned by psychologists as well as by economists and technicians, so that it could be designed to eliminate psychological repression as well as economic repression.[240]

During the 1960s, this style of thinking swept through America and Europe, spread by Fromm, Herbert Marcuse, Norman O. Brown, and other writers favored by the New Left—which combined the left's old demands for economic liberation with a new set of demands for psychological liberation. The "nuclear family" was considered a hotbed of repression and complexes. The ideal was a communal family, loosely knit and undemanding, where everyone helped with the children and there were shifting, multiple sexual relations among adults—very much like what Mead thought she had found in Samoa. Jealousy, possessiveness, or any other form of sexual uptightness was strictly taboo. "Smash monogamy" was as important a slogan as "Smash the state"—almost as important a slogan as "Sex, Drugs, and Rock and Roll!"

When the feminist movement revived during the late 1960s and early 1970s, these ideas about the patriarchal family were at the height of their influence. Feminists attacked many of Freud's ideas, but radical feminists were devout believers in the central Marxist/post-Freudian idea that the patriarchal family is the source of all repression in history. By the 1970s, this theory had matured into "ecofeminism": All through history, patriarchy has been the basis of hierarchical societies that try to dominate people and to conquer nature; we must return to societies based on the feminine values of nurturance of people and of the earth. These ideas are still very influential among some academics and political activists.

Yet the obvious defect of all these theories of patriarchy, from Engels to the modern feminists to the ecofeminists, is that they do not let us criticize new forms of technological control. If you are trying to develop a theory that explains all domination in history, then you will overlook forms of domination that have only become important during the last century. You will overlook the technological domination that will become more and more important in the future.

As If Patriarchy Were the Problem

By the 1960s, the theory of patriarchy was almost completely obsolete.

The word "patriarchy" comes from the Greek word *pater*, meaning "father." It does not mean rule by men: It means rule by fathers, and it has always been used to describe societies organized around the family. Medieval society was patriarchal, for example, because each manor was organized as a sort of extended family, and the lord of the manor had paternal authority over all his subjects. Even as the economy became more developed, it kept many patriarchal features: The workshop of a master craftsman was connected to his home, apprentices lived with his family, and the master had authority over the household.

In the nineteenth century, with the rise of the factory system, this sort of personal relationship became much less important. Instead of personal obligation and obedience, the economy was based on contract and self-interest. Byron wrote before 1820 about the disappearance of patriarchy.[241] The single most important theme of nineteenth-century sociology was that industrialization was causing patriarchal society to be replaced by a more impersonal society.[242]

Yet in the nineteenth and early twentieth centuries, capitalists still did have personal authority over their businesses, and they still resembled fierce, predatory patriarchs; that is why they were called robber barons. In postwar America, as the economy became more bureaucratic, planners and technical experts took over much of the decision making, so gender became less important. When corporate decision makers plug numbers into mathematical models to calculate internal rates of return, it makes no difference at all if they are men or women.

At just the time when patriarchy was disappearing as an organizing principle of our economy, the radicals of the 1960s and 1970s made the attack on "oppressive patriarchal values" the center of their political program. Because they focused on patriarchy, they overlooked forms of domination that are more important to a technological, consumer society. In fact, their attack on patriarchy made them support proposals, such as demands for more day care, which make people more dependent on the technological economy.

A NEW POLITICS

Once upon a time, the attack on the patriarchal family was radical, but it no longer is today. When Engels wrote in the 1880s, it was daring to say that child care should be collective and marriage should last only as long as "sex love" lasts; at the time, it was also daring for a woman to show her ankle. But these ideas are not daring and do not sound appealing today, now that most preschool children are in day care and half of all marriages end in divorce.[243]

Once upon a time, modernism was a radical attack on the traditional institutions that were still the status quo a century ago. But today, modernization itself is the status quo.

A new politics must try to limit modernization to preserve voluntary face-to-face groups. The New Urbanists are doing this by emphasizing the importance of neighborhood: The impersonal housing tracts and shopping centers of modernist urban design are not good enough. And many people on both the left and the right are doing this by focusing on the importance of civil society: The impersonal bureaucracies set up by modernist social programs are not good enough.

The family is also essential. Bureaucratic day-care centers are not good enough.

From Utopia to Anti-Utopia

Some writers did begin to develop a new critique of the modern family. As we have seen, Riesman, Bettelheim, and Lasch showed that the modern family creates exactly the sort of social character needed by modern technological societies.

Oddly enough, these writers who criticized the modern family said many of the same things as the earlier writers who had helped create the modern family. Margaret Mead admitted that the Samoans had shallow feelings, shallow attachments to other people, and little individuality, but she said this was not too high a price to pay for psychological adjustment. The founders of the kibbutz developed their methods of child-raising to avoid the Oedipus complex, and if they had read the authors more closely, they would not have been surprised that their children were very well adjusted but had shallow personalities. You do not need to be a Freudian to understand all this: It is just common sense that children who are brought up in a group, without solitude and without strong attachments to their parents, will grow up into adults who conform to the group, lack inner life, and cannot form strong attachments to other people.

Promoters of modern child-raising early in the century and critics of modern child-raising later in the century agreed that it would have this effect on character. The difference is that the modern family looked appealing early in the century, because it promised to liberate us from the control of patriarchal authority, but it looks frightening today, because it supports the new forms of control used by our technological society.

Aldous Huxley was the first to see that the utopia modern reformers had envisioned early in the twentieth century would turn into an anti-utopia in practice. The society that he described in *Brave New World* was based on modernist ideas about family reform. One of its planners says:

> Freud had been the first to reveal the appalling dangers of family life. . . . And yet, among the savages of Samoa, in certain islands off the coast of New Guinea . . . Home was in any one of twenty palm-thatched houses. In the Trobriands . . . nobody had ever heard of a father.[244]

And he explains that, back when people had only one mother, one father, one husband or wife, their emotions had few outlets, so that "they were forced to feel strongly . . . and strongly, what was more, in solitude, in hopelessly individual isolation"[245] rather than fitting into a smoothly running economic system.

In *Brave New World*, the family had disappeared completely: Children are decanted out of bottles in laboratories and are raised in nurseries and schools, surrounded by other children of the same age. Adults are surrounded by their co-workers all day and spend their time after hours in something like teenage dating; like modern teenagers, they look down on anyone who is different and does not fit in with the crowd. It is considered bad form for adults to have only one sexual partner, because it might lead to too intense an emotional relationship. And solitude is carefully avoided: "People never are alone now. . . . We make them hate solitude; and we arrange their lives so that it's almost impossible for them ever to have it."[246]

The planners once tried to reduce work hours in *Brave New World*, but they found that people could not make use of their own free time and became discontented. Instead, they decided to encourage consumption, in order to give everyone a full day's work. For example, the planners make sure that the games people play in their leisure time require complicated mechanical equipment: They find it shocking that people once played baseball using nothing more elaborate than a ball and a bat—to spend so much time and consume so little!

This society is planned to promote what is called "happiness"—pleasure and the absence of pain or disturbance—and the idea that there might be some higher purpose in life would threaten social stability. Older views of ethics have to be suppressed because "Mass production demanded the shift. Universal happiness keeps the wheels steadily turning; truth and beauty can't."[247]

The left's attacks on the patriarchal family, from Engels to Fromm to the ecofeminists, assumes that the greatest threats to freedom are authoritarian fathers who control their children and the authoritarian governments that are rooted psychologically in this sort of family. But in a modern technological economy, the real danger is that society will be planned and organized to insure everyone's "happiness," and that people will be so completely absorbed by society—so much a part of the group from earliest childhood on—that they will lack the inner life needed to think for themselves about what happiness really is. They will not even want shorter work hours, because they lack the self-discipline and the inner life that is needed to make good use of their own free time.

The family is the best protection against this sort of technocratic control. Strong families that give the youngest children solitude by taking care of them at home and that actively form older children's characters are essential to creating inner life and inner direction.

A Sustainable Society

The therapeutic state and the growth economy no longer work. If we are going to move toward a sustainable society and economy, the family will have to change as dramatically in the future as it did during the past two centuries. The family was transformed by modernization, and it must be transformed again as we move beyond the age of economic growth.

In traditional economies, families and local communities did virtually all the productive work. The home and neighborhood economy was still intact in most of America during the early nineteenth century, when families grew their own food and built their own homes of logs or sod.

During the nineteenth and early twentieth centuries, the money economy took over many functions of the home economy, but the family still had important economic functions. Though material production began to move into factories, the home was still responsible for cooking, washing, sewing, and other productive work. Most entertainment was also homemade: Families played parlor games or read out loud, and middle-class women were expected to know how to play the piano. Most important, the family and the local community were responsible for raising children, for helping the poor, and for other caring activities. Yet the home economy was women's work, so it was valued less highly than men's work in the money economy.

In postwar America, for the first time, people believed that the home had no real productive role, that it was purely a center for consumption. The money economy had taken over almost all material production. Rather than entertaining themselves, families sat in front of the television to be amused by what we call the entertainment industry. The welfare state had taken over the responsibility for charity. And the schools and nursery schools had taken over most of the responsibility for raising children. The product that defined the spirit of the time was the "TV dinner": The idea was that families would be better off eating these mass-produced dinners, so that they would have more time to watch television.

It was a time of technological optimism. Everyone assumed that economic growth could make people more and more prosperous indefinitely. And everyone assumed that the money economy could take over all the work of the home economy—that technology would do this work better than the home ever had.

Today, we can see that endless economic growth is not sustainable: Worldwide concern about resource depletion and about environmental problems such as global warming has made it clear that we have to limit growth for ecological reasons. Just as important, we have to limit growth for social reasons: High rates of crime and suicide among teenagers, the breakdown of civil society, the damage done by high divorce rates, and many other symptoms of increasing anomie have all made it clear that the money economy cannot completely replace the community and home.

Today, our most extreme radicals want to scrap the industrial economy and return to an economy where people build their own houses, raise their own food, and home-birth and home-school their own children. During the 1970s, the appropriate technology movement said we should use small-scale machines for local production. Now, things have gone even further:

Some radical ecologists have taken to calling themselves Luddites, after the weavers who smashed the power looms in early-nineteenth-century England.[248] Both these movements emphasize that production for local use is needed not only to preserve the natural environment but also to preserve the home and community.

We obviously will not abandon industrialization, but we do need to limit economic growth and give people more free time to do for themselves, in order to restore some balance between the money economy and the home economy. As extreme and impractical as they are, the new Luddites are important because they are pointing toward a new political direction that in many ways is just the opposite of socialism and other modernist doctrines.

It is most practical for the home economy to take back the work that it has lost most recently. The new Luddites want homesteads and small-scale machinery to take back the work that factories took over during the nineteenth century, but this is not practical in economically advanced countries: In general, factories took over because they are far more efficient than home production. The automobile took over our transportation system more recently, but it *is* practical to rebuild our neighborhoods so people can walk: The automobile took over not because it is efficient—it is much less efficient than public transportation—but because it was considered a luxury consumer good. Now, we can see that cities where people can walk are far more livable; but rebuilding our cities around the automobile took many decades, and rebuilding them around the pedestrian will also take many decades. It is only recently that the money economy has taken child care away from the home economy, and people could take this work back now, if we had the political will.

If we limited growth, people would use some of their free time for gardening, crafts, and other material production, but this sort of home production will never be as important as industrial production: Freshly baked bread, hand-made furniture, and home-grown vegetables are better than industrial products, but the mass-produced versions are much cheaper and are good enough for most purposes. It is most important for the home and neighborhood economy to take back the work that the money economy cannot do well: making good use of our free time, running voluntary organizations in our communities, raising our children.

THE HOMEMAKER AS ROLE MODEL

This new political direction should change feminism, just as radically as modernism changed it a century ago. In fact, some ecologically oriented feminist thinkers are already calling for this sort of social and economic change.

For example, Marilyn Waring, a feminist economist and environmental and peace activist from New Zealand, began to develop what she calls a "new feminist economics" when she saw that economic development in the third world damaged the natural environment and local subsistence economies. She found that the United Nations System of National Accounts, developed to measure economic progress in the third world, encouraged this damage, because it did not account for the value of the environment or for the value of subsistence labor, which was usually done by women. Working in the developing nations, Waring realized that conventional economics, which only looks at the value of the money economy, did not count the things she cared about most.[249]

Barbara Brandt, a feminist writer and social change activist, makes the same point about the American economy. Economic growth has expanded what she calls the formal economy at the expense of the natural environment and of the informal economy of the home and community. The formal economy is traditionally the masculine realm, its producers work for other people, its goal is efficiency and profit, and it serves only those who can pay. The informal economy is traditionally the feminine realm, its producers work for themselves, its goal is to fill immediate needs, and it serves everyone, including dependent people who cannot pay. Because the informal economy is small scale and voluntary, Brandt says, it is more responsive to needs and more personally fulfilling and empowering than the money economy.[250]

The Finnish feminist economist Hilkka Pietila calls large profit-making businesses "the fettered economy"—though this is usually called the free-market economy. And the work people do voluntarily, without being paid, for the well-being of their families or communities or for their own pleasure, she calls "the free economy."[251]

These writers are pointing toward a new direction for feminism. Modern feminists were taken in by the technological optimism of the twentieth century. Early in the century, feminists said that that women must "follow their work out of the home," because it was inevitable that the modern money economy would take over all the functions of the home economy, and during the 1960s and 1970s, feminists encouraged women to get jobs in the modern economy. But today we must replace this modernist version of feminism with a new feminism that recognizes the limits of modernization and growth.

When the Industrial Revolution first began to displace subsistence economies, men were forced into the money economy, but women continued traditional forms of production for use. Now that we need to find a better balance between the money economy and the household and community economy, the housewife is a useful role model for both men and women—not the housewife of the 1950s, who was bored because she was stuck in the home with nothing important to do, but the Victorian house-wife, who did essential unpaid work in her home, in her neighborhood, and in voluntary organizations.

All of us—men and women—can learn from the work that women did during the nineteenth and early twentieth centuries, when men had been absorbed into the money economy but the home economy still had vital-ity. Women still produced for use at home: They cooked, washed, mended, and did other economically necessary work. Even this sort of routine house-work, though it is tedious, is more satisfying than a routine factory job, because you perform a meaningful task from beginning to end under your own direction. But middle-class women also did more interesting work in community and cultural organizations: They volunteered at churches, charities, and other community groups, they ran literary societies, they were expected to know how to play the piano, and they raised the children.

American men still took all these activities seriously at the beginning of the nineteenth century, but when the Industrial Revolution came, men turned this work over to women. In colonial America, most men worked at home, but after industrialization took hold, women's work at home was not considered as important as the work men did for money. In colonial America, literary and scientific societies were common; Benjamin Franklin was a member of a literary group when he was a young man, and he retired from business when he was in his 40s, so that he could devote his time to politics and science. It was not until later in the nineteenth century that Americans began to feel that "ladies' literary societies" were not as serious as men's business affairs. In colonial America, men were also in charge of raising and disciplining the children.

The Industrial Revolution started earlier in England. At the end of the seventeenth century, John Locke wrote that men should not learn to play musical instruments, because it "wastes so much of a young man's time to give him but a moderate skill in it."[252] Women should cultivate this "accomplishment" to please their families, but men should devote their time to the serious business of making money. As England became the world's greatest economic power, it stopped producing great music: Until the twentieth century, there was not an important English-born musician after Henry Purcell, who died in 1696. But today, we can stop listening to Locke's advice. We have made enough money, and we can take some time to make music again.

Women led the way in gaining free time during the nineteenth cen-tury. Men's work hours declined slowly before 1900, and it was not quite legitimate for men to want free time: Though workingmen said privately that they wanted shorter hours so they could have time for their families and for do-it-yourself projects, union leaders argued publicly that shorter hours would make them more efficient workers. Married women's participation in the money economy declined more quickly, because everyone agreed it was legitimate for women to have more time for their families, homes, and communities.

Modernist Feminism

We owe thanks to the feminists of the 1960s and 1970s for insisting that women are fully human and should have lives of their own, rather than living for their husbands and children. Before that time, both men and women were diminished by narrow gender roles. Men worked at nine-to-five jobs and did not have enough time for their children or their own interests. Women were confined to the home, and their interests were not taken as seriously as they should have been. Both men and women live fuller lives when they take some responsibility for necessary economic work, which used to be the man's sphere, and also take some responsibility for home, children, community, and cultural activities, which were devalued during the nineteenth century because they were the woman's sphere.

But modernists wanted women to escape their traditional roles by entering the money economy, and they rejected the home economy completely. This idea began with nineteenth-century socialists, who believed that modernization would collectivize all the work that was done at home. It spread in the early twentieth century, as progressives argued that women would inevitably follow their work out of the home. It changed American society during the past few decades, when women entered the workforce en masse. Americans devalued the home and community economy more completely than ever before.

The mainstream women's movement still turns its back on the family and community economy. For example, the National Organization for Women (NOW) does not talk about flexible work hours—no doubt because they believe that new mothers would take advantage of them more often than fathers, so it would slow women's advancement in their careers.[253] They ignore any value that conflicts with women's advancement in the money economy.

The left has lost its influence because it has not abandoned the modernist vision of the future, though even it finds this technological future increasingly bleak. For example, Hillary Clinton writes:

> Where we used to chat with neighbors on stoops and porches, now we watch videos in our darkened living rooms. Instead of strolling down Main Street, we spend hours in automobiles and at anonymous shopping malls. We don't

join civic association, churches, unions, political parties, or even bowling leagues the way we used to. . . . To many, this brave new world seems dehumanizing and inhospitable. It is not surprising, then, that there is a yearning for the "good old days" as a refuge from the problems of the present. But by turning away, we blind ourselves to the continuing, evolving presence of the village in our lives.[254]

In her "evolving" village, it is inevitable that federally funded therapeutic programs will take over the work that used to be done by the family and community. Apparently, Mrs. Clinton has not heard that the New Urbanists are now building neighborhoods where people can walk to Main Street and sit on their front porches,[255] and that both conservatives and liberals are now talking about how to revive civil society.

Yet for all her faith in the therapeutic state, she cannot free herself of the thought that her proposals do not deal with the real problems of modern society—which she herself calls a dehumanizing, inhospitable brave new world. Isn't it amazing that someone who considers herself a progressive working for social change really believes that nothing can be done to change modern society significantly?

A New Feminism

Modernist feminism has lost its influence as the failings of modernization have become apparent. Today, everyone can see that the decline of the family and of civil society is a problem, and it seems that feminists have contributed to this decline by rejecting women's traditional role in the home and community.

A new feminism should do just the opposite. It should work to limit the money economy and to reclaim a role in the family and community for both men and women.

Feminists can regain their influence if they stop fighting yesterday's battles against traditional society and start looking at the new problems of modern society. In the modern economy, specialized organizations run by experts have taken over all the activities that people used to manage for themselves. In modern families, both parents work full time. The children are in day care, school, or extended care full time. The grandparents are in a "leisure living" retirement village that manages their recreation, and then in a long-term medical facility that manages their death. The question is how we can move beyond the traditional family and its narrowly defined roles without moving toward this sort of modern family, which is totally unable to do for itself.

A feminist movement that criticized modern society would not reject women's traditional work in the home and community in favor of careers in the money economy. Instead, it would want to limit economic growth, in order to give men and women more free time for work in the home and community. Rather than demanding more day-care and after-school programs to help women succeed in their careers, it would create a new definition of success for both men and women, a more balanced definition of success.

The home and community were gradually devalued during the nineteenth and twentieth centuries, but to move beyond the age of economic growth, we need a better balance between the money economy and the home and community economy. This means that both men and women should be able to do the work that makes best use of their talents. They should not be limited by narrowly defined gender roles. And they also should not be limited by the idea that men's traditional work for money is more important than women's traditional work in the home and community.

The current generation of feminist writers grew up in the 1950s and 1960s, when Ozzie and Harriet families were the norm, and they are still fighting old battles. But you cannot live in the past forever. When we have a new generation of writers who grew up in families with working parents, two cars, and no free time, feminists will stop attacking the traditional family and start trying to change the modern family.

LOOKING BACK FROM 2030

In reality, people will probably look back in the year 2030 and see that consumerism continued to spread, that global warming and energy shortages kept getting worse despite repeated technological fixes, and that there is a desperate need for real socioeconomic change. But let's take a moment to imagine how our children and grandchildren could look back on us in a few decades if we come to our senses and start to make the needed changes now.

In the year 2030, Heather and Mark are both in their 30s. They have been married for 10 years, and they have two children, 9-year-old Mary and 4-year-old James. Mark works 20 hours a week as a forklift operator, and Heather works 25 hours a week as a secretary but is allowed to telecommute partially and work 8 of those hours at home.

They can get by on their income, because of the extra money they get from the dependent tax credit and, more important, the child-care tax credit that they get for taking care of James at home—since the child-care credit for low- and moderate-income people is equivalent to almost $10,000 per year in our dollars. In 2 years, when James starts school, they will both have to increase their work hours—unlike better-paid professional couples, who usually manage to keep it down to 40 hours a week between them, even after their children are in school—but one of them will always be home with the children after school.

They own a small house in a neighborhood developed in the 2020s, about the same size as the bungalows that were popular among moderate-income homebuyers during the 1920s, though it is in a more traditional style, with a large front porch. Heather commutes to her job downtown on the new light-rail line, and Mark usually bicycles to work. They do most of their shopping on Central Avenue, which is only a two-block walk from their house. Their daughter Mary is proud that she has just started walking to a local elementary school "by herself," rather than having a parent walk with her—although she actually walks with another girl who lives on the block. Both Heather and Mark like walking with James to the local tot-park, a block and a half away, where he always finds some of his neighborhood friends to play with; and they also like to walk with him to the local coffee shop, three blocks away, where they always find some neighborhood friends to talk with, sitting on the ledge while James plays in the planters in front. They find that they only use their car occasionally, when the weather is bad or when they go on weekend drives or other special trips; in fact, the old 2017 Insight Hybrid that they bought used 10 years ago has only 60,000 miles on it and is still running fine.

How do they feel when they look back on how their parents lived when they were small children? They both grew up in edge-city subdivisions, on twisting streets of identical houses with two-car garages, where you had to drive on the freeway to get to the nearest shopping mall. Their houses were not as big as the "McMansions" that became popular among professional people during the 1990s, but they were bigger than the modest bungalow they live in now. They both had working-class parents who were stretched financially and needed two full-time jobs just to pay the bills, and neither of them can remember a time when they were not put in day care all day. Mark was devastated by his parents' divorce when he was in sixth grade.

Both Heather and Mark were swept up in the widespread revulsion against the vicious circle of overworking and overspending, which began early in the twenty-first century and led to a new emphasis on home and family. Changes in the law came quickly—for example, the child-care tax credit and laws promoting flexible work hours. Changes in people's habits came more slowly: It took decades of rebuilding before most Americans lived in walkable neighborhoods, but by now, the neighborhoods Heather and Mark grew up in, like many of the sprawling suburbs built around the freeways during the twentieth century, have been abandoned by residents and restored as farmland and parks.

Heather and Mark have the usual reaction when they look back at the overspent and overworked America they grew up in. They regret how much they missed during their own childhood, and they are determined that their own children will not have the same regrets. About their parents' generation, more than anything else, they feel sorry that they wasted so much time making and spending money that they missed out on the real satisfactions of life. (Fortunately, the country began to reject consumerism before the environmental damage was irreversible: If the consumer economy had kept charging ahead for a few more decades and done permanent damage, people would look back on it with anger rather than with pity.)

Their parents had no spare time to do anything after work except to sit in front of the television relaxing, but Mark and Heather have both made good use of the time that they spend at home with their children.

Mark coaches the local children's soccer teams—one of the many dedicated soccer moms and dads in the neighborhood. And he has always enjoyed working on their house: He started by remodeling the kitchen, then he redid the exterior woodwork, and then he built a stone barbecue pit in the backyard. Then he began carving a custom front door for the house, and when he was done, he was surprised that the word spread and other people in the neighborhood asked if he would carve custom doors for them. Now he has a small business carving doors; the children love to watch him and help when they can, and he enjoys the work even though he earns less than a dollar an hour.[256]

Heather found that she enjoyed the books she read to her children as much as they did, and now she volunteers in the library of her daughter's school one afternoon a week. She also has played guitar ever since she was a child. She kept up this skill by playing at home, and both children have learned to play a bit. A couple of years ago, she started a band with a few friends, similar to the band she was in during her high school years; they sometimes play at local restaurants, and they sell their music over the Internet. We cannot imagine what this future music is like, but we can be sure that it is much less driven and less frantic than the music their parents and grandparents listened to back in the late twentieth century.

AFTERWORD:
A PERSONAL NOTE

In this book, I have cited the relevant literature and Census Bureau statistics, but I also have a more personal interest in the subject. For 5 years, until my son started school, I was what is sometimes called a "househusband": My wife worked while I stayed home.

In part, this was an economic decision: At the time, my wife was earning more than I was. And in part, it was because I believed that the work I did to earn money was not as vital or as important as the work I would be doing by staying home.

There were many wonderful moments. Every day, I used to make wheat-germ pancakes for lunch and count as I scooped out the flour, and I can remember very well how exciting it was the first time that I said "one, two," and my son said "fwee" before I could finish. When he got a bit older, we could not walk a few blocks without his challenging me to a race, and rather than moving both arms back and forth as he ran, he used to swing his left arm around and around in a circle. Best of all, sometimes I was able to see the world through his eyes—to look up at the backyards of the houses as we walked by on the sidewalk and see how big and mysterious and magical each one was.

I had the time to do other things, too. I became active in community affairs for the first time. I began by forming a small political group working on transportation issues and, after a couple of years, I was appointed to the Transportation Commission. Since most political organizing is done over the phone, this was a perfect project for spare moments at home.

My wife always insisted on taking over child care as soon as she got home from work, and so I had the evenings free. I not only went to political meetings, I also began taking computer courses in the evening. After my son started school, I was able to find computer work that I could do at home, so someone was there when he came home from school.

But it was hard to get by economically before I started working. Because of California's high housing costs, we had to rent the lower unit of a single-family home that had been divided into two flats: our bedroom was a tiny room that used to be the sun porch, and the baby slept in what used to be the dining room, which we had to curtain off from the living room. At the time, our friends who put their children in day care were buying houses, but we were not able to afford a house until after I went back to work.

When my son became a teenager, his friends began to phone him and say that they wanted to come over and visit because they were bored. For a while, "Hello—I'm bored" was the most common message on our answering machine. My son couldn't understand it, because he was always starting projects that took up all his spare time.

When he was 11 or 12, he became interested in knife making: He would design knives and make patterns for them out of paper. Once he decided which one to make, I would cut its general shape out of sheet metal, and then he would use a grinder to shape it more exactly and sharpen it. Now, he still makes knives, he cuts the sheet metal himself, and he lectures us on the properties of different types of metals. But he has become even more interested in natural fibers and foods. He can identify the local plants, he knows which are useful for fiber and uses them to make rope, and he dug up our entire frontyard so he could plant desert plants that are useful for food and fiber. These are all interests that he developed on his own—things that he now knows much more about than I do.

When his friends used to call and say they were bored, I asked him whether they liked to make things, the way he did. He answered, in a bit of a puzzled tone, that all they liked to do was listen to music and watch television. This sounds to me like more anecdotal evidence that, if children have some solitude and time to themselves when they are infants, they will also be able to make use of their own time when they get older.

My only regret is that it goes by so quickly. When you are a child, it seems to take forever to grow up. But when you are an adult, your children seem to grow up almost instantly. Yet most people today are so busy earning a living that they cannot take advantage of the bit of time that they do have with their children.

NOTES

The opening quote from Senator Mikulski appeared in the *San Francisco Chronicle* of June 15, 1987.

PREFACE

1. Kirstin Downey Grimsley, "Young Men Value Family Above Career, Poll Shows," *San Francisco Chronicle*, May 3, 2000, p. A7. According to this poll, done by Harris Interactive for the Radcliffe Public Policy Center, 70 percent of men in their 20s and 63 percent of women in their 20s are willing to give up pay in exchange for more time with their families. By contrast, only 26 percent of men over 65 said they would give up pay in exchange for more time with their families, compared with 69 percent of women over 65.

CHAPTER 1

2. Juliet Schor, *The Overworked American: The Unexpected Decline of Leisure* (New York: Basic Books, 1991), pp. 84–85.

3. *World Watch* magazine, May/June 1999.

4. According to one recent study, the elasticity of vehicle miles traveled with respect to highway lane miles in California is 0.9 at the metropolitan level within

5 years. In other words, 5 years after a major metropolitan freeway is completed, 90 percent of its capacity is taken up by vehicle trips that would not have occurred if the road had not been built. Mark Hansen and Yuanlin Huang, "Road Supply and Traffic in California Urban Areas," *Transportation Research A* 31, no. 3 (March 1997): 205–218.

5. For example, a 1995 study by the Families and Work Institute shows that only 15 percent of working women with school-age children want to work full time, although 75 percent currently do so. Sylvia Ann Hewlett and Cornel West, *The War Against Parents* (Boston: Houghton Mifflin, 1998), p. 107. Likewise, a survey of 50,000 Americans conducted by *Family Circle* magazine found that two-thirds would prefer to care for their own children: reported in *Money*, July 1988: 95. Another poll found that 80 percent would prefer to care for their own children: reported in the *San Francisco Chronicle*, May 17, 1989, p. Z6.

6. This is the maximum credit allowed for families with an adjusted gross income over $28,000 and with two or more children. Lower-income families are allowed a bit more.

7. Yet child-care policies do have a measurable effect on growth. According to one study, because child-care tax credits encourage women to enter the labor market, our annual GNP is as much as $8.4 billion higher than it would be without these tax credits. David R. Henderson, *Child Care Tax Credits: A Supply-Side Success Story*, National Center for Policy Analysis Policy Report No. 140, July 1989.

8. During the 1970s and 1980s, White children lost 10 hours a week of parental time, while Black children lost 12 hours. Hewlett and West, *War Against Parents*, p. 48.

9. Per-capita GNP in constant 1992 dollars was $12,512 in 1960 and $25,615 in 1995. Just as significant, per-capita personal consumption expenditures in constant 1992 dollars were $7,926 in 1960 and $17,403 in 1995, so personal consumption has much more than doubled. U.S. Bureau of the Census, *Statistical Abstract of the United States, 1996,* 116th ed. (Washington, D.C.: U.S. Government Printing Office, 1996), p. 448.

To compare 1920 with 1995, we need to use historical as well as recent statistics. Per-capita GNP in constant 1958 dollars was $1,315 in 1920 and $3,555 in 1970. U.S. Bureau of the Census, *Historical Statistics of the United States, Colonial Times to 1970*, bicentennial ed. (Washington, D.C.: U.S. Government Printing Office, 1975), p. 224. Per-capita GNP in constant 1992 dollars was $16,520 in 1970 and $25,615 in 1995. Census, *Statistical Abstract, 1996*. In total, then, per-capita GNP in 1995 was over four times as much in real terms as per-capita GNP in 1920.

10. John Kenneth Galbraith, *The Affluent Society* (Boston: Houghton Mifflin, 1958). Vance Packard, *The Waste Makers* (New York, David McKay, 1960). These were just the most famous books about the affluence and wastefulness of the American economy, and there were also many others, such as John Keats, *The Insolent Chariots* (New York: Lippincott, 1958), about Americans' excessive use of the automobile, and Martin Mayer, *Madison Avenue, U.S.A.* (New York: Harper, 1958), about the excesses of the advertising industry.

11.   Betty Friedan, *The Feminine Mystique* (New York: Dell, 1977, originally published 1963), p. 28 *et seq.*

CHAPTER 2

12.   Census, *Statistical Abstract, 1996*, p. 400.

13.   The divorce rate was 2.2 per 1,000 population in 1960 and 5.2 per 1,000 in 1980. U.S. Bureau of the Census, *Statistical Abstract of the United States, 1985*, 105th ed. (Washington, D.C.: U.S. Government Printing Office, 1985), p. 80.

14.   To be more precise, the divorce rate has declined since 1980, but the marriage rate has also declined. In 1980, there were 10.6 marriages and 5.2 divorces per 1,000 population, and in 1994, there were 9.1 marriages and 4.6 divorces per 1,000 population. Census, *Statistical Abstract, 1996*, p. 107. The divorce rate has decreased since 1980, but the number of divorces as a percentage of the number of marriages has increased very slightly. After 1996, the marriage rate began to increase and the divorce rate continued to decline, but these encouraging statistics are a bit misleading, because the rate of first marriages has not increased—only the rate of remarriages. In addition, as David Popenoe points out, the decreased marriage rate has gone along with an increased rate of cohabitation; although there are not reliable figures, it seems likely that the overall instability of households has increased significantly, since cohabitation is generally much less stable than marriage. David Popenoe, *Life Without Father: Compelling New Evidence That Fatherhood and Marriage Are Indispensable for the Good of Children and Society* (Cambridge, Mass.: Harvard University Press, 1996), p. 20.

15.   McLanahan and Sandefur, *Growing Up with a Single Parent: What Hurts, What Helps* (Cambridge, Mass.: Harvard University Press, 1994), p. 2.

16.   The figures are even more disturbing when we break them down by race. Among children born in 1980, 70 percent of White children and 94 percent of Black children spend at least part of their childhood living with a single parent. Popenoe, *Life Without Father*, p. 22.

17.   Ibid., p. 81.

18.   Dolores Hayden, *The Grand Domestic Revolution: A History of Feminist Designs for American Homes, Neighborhoods, and Cities* (Cambridge, Mass.: MIT Press, 1981), p. 55.

19.   Popenoe, *Life Without Father*, p. 97.

20.   In England and Wales, illegitimacy declined from almost 7 percent of all births in the 1840s to less than 4 percent in 1901, and the crime rate from almost 500 per 100,000 population in 1857 to about 250 in 1901. There are no national figures in the United States during this period, but the local figures that are available indicate that similar declines occurred here. Gertrude Himmelfarb, *The Demoralization of Society: From Victorian Virtues to Modern Values* (New York: Vintage, 1996), pp. 226–232.

21.   Hayden, *Grand Domestic Revolution*, p. 16.

22.   Edward Bellamy, *Looking Backward, 2000–1887* (Boston: Ticknor & Company, 1888).

23. Frances Willard, quoted in Hayden, *Grand Domestic Revolution*, p. 5.

24. For example, she wrote in *Women and Economics*, "To take from any community its male workers would paralyze it economically to a far greater degree than to remove its female workers. The labor now performed by women could be performed by the men, requiring only the setting back of many advanced workers into earlier forms of industry.... Man can cook, clean and sew as well as women; but the making and managing of the great engines of modern industry, the threading of the earth and sea in our vast systems of transportation, the handling of our elaborate machinery of trade, commerce and government,—these things could not be done so well by women in their present degree of economic development." (Notice that there is no mention of raising children.) Charlotte Perkins Gilman, *The Yellow Wallpaper and Other Writings* (reprint, New York: Bantam, 1989), pp. 136–137.

25. Hayden, *Grand Domestic Revolution*, p. 195.

26. Ibid., p. 16.

27. Ibid., p. 226.

28. Ibid., p. 14.

29. Prefatory Letter from Theodore Roosevelt, Mrs. John Van Vorst and Marie Van Vorst, *The Woman Who Toils* (New York: Doubleday, Page & Co, 1903), p. vii.

30. A letter from Roosevelt to Cecil Spring Rice, cited by Christopher Lasch, *Haven in a Heartless World: The Family Besieged* (New York: Basic Books, 1978a), p. 8.

31. Popenoe, *Life Without Father*, p. 116.

32. Ibid., p. 28.

33. Ibid., p. 29.

34. In 1966, a man who had stolen $5 worth of candy when he was 16 years old won a suit against the state of New York, which had confined him in a mental hospital for 41 years; the authorities refused to release him, because they said he had "delusions of persecution" that they had not yet treated successfully. The court ruled that the man did not have delusions at all, that the hospital really had persecuted him. This is one of the first cases where the courts rejected the theory that people did not need or have any rights if the state was "helping" them. Thomas Szasz, *Ideology and Insanity: Essays on the Psychiatric Dehumanization of Man* (Garden City, N.Y.: Doubleday Anchor, 1970), p. 106.

35. Lasch, *Haven*, p. 14.

36. Philippe Ariès, *Centuries of Childhood: A Social History of Family Life*, trans. Robert Baldick (New York: Vintage, 1962), p. 21.

37. Barbara Kaye Greenleaf, *Children Through the Ages: A History of Childhood* (New York: Barnes & Noble, 1978), p. 53.

38. A pamphlet published in 1730 by Thomas Chalkey, quoted in J. William Frost, *The Quaker Family* (New York: St. Martin's Press, 1973), p. 74.

39. They were first developed earlier in the nineteenth century but did not become popular until around the turn of the twentieth century, spurred by the model kindergarten shown at the Columbian Exposition of 1892–1893. The first kindergarten, for children between ages 3 and 7, was opened in 1837 in Blankenberg, Thuringia, by the German educator Froedrich Froebel.

40. Talcott Parsons, Robert F. Bales, et al., *Family: Socialization and Interaction Process* (Glencoe, Ill.: Free Press, 1955), p. 25.

41. See, for example, "Individualism Reconsidered" in David Riesman, *Individualism Reconsidered and Other Essays* (Glencoe, Ill.: Free Press, 1954), and the most famous of these books, William H. Whyte, *The Organization Man* (New York: Simon & Schuster, 1956).

42. This name was invented in a best-selling book of social criticism, Phillip Wylie, *A Generation of Vipers* (New York: Farrar & Rinehart, 1942). During the 1950s, "momism" became a commonplace among students of the American family: It was such a popular idea that it made it into the movie *Rebel Without a Cause,* where James Dean walks out in disgust when his father tries to talk to him while washing the dishes wearing a frilly woman's apron.

43. John R. Seeley, R. Alexander Sim, and Elizabeth W. Loosley, *Crestwood Heights: A Study of the Culture of Suburban Life* (New York: Basic Books, 1956), p. 164.

44. Nena O'Neill and George O'Neill, *Open Marriage: A New Life Style for Couples* (New York: M. Evans & Company, 1972).

45. Mel Krantzler, *Creative Divorce: A New Opportunity for Personal Growth* (New York: New American Library: Signet Books, 1975).

46. During the 1950s and 1960s, studies that showed the damage done by single parenthood were based on samples that were small and also biased; for example, they looked at children who were being treated for psychological problems or who were wards of the court. In 1973, Elizabeth Herzog and Cecelia Sudia did a review of the research, which showed that these studies had methodological failings and did not prove that single motherhood was bad for children. Many leftist academics used this review as proof that single-parent families had no negative consequences—though it actually just showed that there was no good research on the subject. McLanahan and Sandefur, *Growing Up with a Single Parent,* pp. 13–14. Of course, the academic community was eager to take this position: It had already taken it at the time of the Moynihan Report, when even this review of the research did not exist.

47. "[T]he controversy surrounding the Moynihan report had the effect of curtailing serious research on minority problems in the inner city for over a decade, as liberal scholars shied away from researching behavior construed as unflattering or stigmatizing to particular racial minorities." William Julius Wilson, *The Truly Disadvantaged: The Inner City, the Underclass, and Public Policy* (Chicago: University of Chicago Press, 1990), p. 4.

48. See Popenoe, *Life Without Father,* pp. 60–61.

49. See Judith Wallerstein and Sandra Blakeslee, *Second Chances* (New York: Ticknor & Fields, 1989). Wallerstein studied 60 couples from affluent, suburban Marin County (California)who divorced in 1971, and she first published her results in 1980. Her study has been criticized for not having a control group and for possible biases in its sampling, but despite any methodological problems, it was an important wake-up call that led to the more definitive statistical studies of divorce of the 1980s and 1990s.

50. Popenoe, *Life Without Father,* p. 35.

51. Ibid., pp. 30–31.

52. Robert Bellah, Richard Madsen, William Sullivan, Ann Swidler, and Steven Tipton, *Habits of the Heart: Individualism and Commitment in American Life* (New York: Harper & Row, 1985), p. 101.

53. At the Robert Taylor Homes, a complex of 28 sixteen-story buildings that is Chicago's largest housing project, 93 percent of households with children were headed by unwed mothers by 1980. The official population of the project was 20,000 people, but it was estimated that there were an additional 5,000 to 7,000 residents who were not registered with the housing authority. The total number of residents was less than 1 percent of Chicago's population, but in 1980, 11 percent of Chicago's murders, 9 percent of rapes, and 10 percent of aggravated assaults occurred in this project. Wilson, *The Truly Disadvantaged*, p. 25.

54. McLanahan and Sandefur, *Growing Up with a Single Parent*, p. 42.

55. Ibid., p. 49.

56. Ibid., pp. 53–54. This figure applies to women born after 1953.

57. Ibid., p. 82.

58. Ibid., pp. 79–95.

59. For the best summary of the research, see Popenoe, *Life Without Father*, particularly pp. 52–78. Another good summary of the research is in Barbara Dafoe Whitehead, "Dan Quayle Was Right," *Atlantic Monthly*, April 1993, pp. 47 *et seq.* See also Barbara Dafoe Whitehead, *The Divorce Culture* (New York: Knopf, 1997), and David Blankenhorn, *Fatherless America: Confronting Our Most Urgent Social Problem* (New York: Basic Books, 1995).

60. Popenoe, *Life Without Father*, p. 62.

61. Ibid., p. 9.

62. *San Francisco Chronicle*, September 14, 1999, p. A3.

63. George Gilder is well known for his best-selling book *Wealth and Poverty* (New York: Basic Books, 1981), which was a favorite of President Reagan, but he began by writing books with more lurid titles about men's need to dominate their families: *Sexual Suicide* (New York: Quadrangle, 1973) and *Naked Nomads: Unmarried Men in America* (New York: Quadrangle/New York Times Books, 1974). After he became famous, *Sexual Suicide* was republished under the more sober title *Men and Marriage* (Pelican, 1986).

64. Judith Stacey, *Brave New Families* (New York: Basic Books, 1991), p. 253. Her more recent book makes essentially the same point; see Judith Stacey, *In the Name of the Family: Rethinking Family Values in the Postmodern Age* (Boston: Beacon 1996).

65. Stacey, *Brave New Families*, p. 269. She adds that "All democratic people . . . should work to hasten [the family's] demise. An ideological concept that imposes mythical homogeneity on the diverse means by which people organize their intimate relationships, 'the family' distorts and devalues the rich variety of kinship stories." Of course, you could say the same thing about any ideal: Stacey is against racism and sexism, but the ideal of equality that she espouses is also an ideological concept that imposes homogeneity on people's intimate relationships and devalues the rich variety of stories that they tell about gender and race.

66. Laura Hagar, "The American Family Is Dead! Long Live American Families" (an interview with Judith Stacey), *The Express* (San Francisco), February 21, 1997, p. 1, pp. 6–13.

67. See Stephanie Coontz, *The Way We Never Were: American Families and the Nostalgia Trap* (New York: Basic Books, 1992) and *The Way We Really Are: Coming to Terms with America's Changing Families* (New York: Basic Books, 1997).

68. Hewlett and West, *War on Parents*, seems to be the current favorite on the academic left. Hewlett and West are right to decry the breakdown of the American family rather than defending it as a postmodern experiment in diversity, but their solution to the breakdown of the family is a return to the suburban affluence of the 1950s.

They write that the 1950s were the "golden age of the American family" (p. 97). One reason is that "the economy was moving along at an impressive clip, doubling every ten years, and most people participated in the expanding affluence" (p. 63) so that the economic "progress of this era become the stuff of the American Dream" (p. 63).

The government also promoted the affluence of 1950s families. Congress expanded tax breaks for mortgages, and FHA regulations made sure these tax breaks went to young married couples moving to suburban homes (p. 99). The GI Bill jump-started the boom: "Most of these units were in suburban subdivisions like Levittown, on Long Island, where the new government subsidies brought a single-family home within the reach of most returning veterans. In just five years, from 1950 to 1954, the suburban rings around American cities increased their population by 35 percent" (p. 102). Families' "housing needs" were also subsidized by the 1950s "Highway Act" (p. 34), which made it easier for them to get to the suburbs—presumably the Interstate Highway Act, which funded an explosion of freeway construction.

Hewlett and West admit that Levittown had some problems, such as excluding Blacks (p. 102), but it is odd that they glorify the 1950s vision of suburbia at all, at a time when the New Urbanists have become successful by arguing that it weakens the sense of community and damages the environment. And it is odd that they can glorify the 1950s rapid economic growth, at a time when environmentalists are arguing that growth threatens us with global warming and resource depletion. They are trying to forge a new direction for progressive politics, but they ignore these key issues.

Hewlett and West want to create a new self-interest group to demand higher income and more programs for parents, as the American Association of Retired Persons (AARP) does for older people, so they conclude their book with a hodgepodge of demands that does not add up to a coherent vision of the future. They also want an end to economic stagnation: Higher incomes for parents is a keystone of their program.

But sometimes their own arguments show that hard economic times are not really the cause of the family's decline. For example, they say "in 1959, 20 percent of families with children were poor. . . . More than three decades later, in 1993, the child poverty rate among families with children stood at 19 percent, barely changed from its 1959 level" (p. 121). We certainly should do more to reduce child poverty, but it is hard to accept their constant claims that poverty is a major cause of families' problems—for example, that it is the key cause of child abuse (p. 117)—when the poverty rate today is a bit lower than it was in the "golden age" of the 1950s.

In an even more striking example, they describe a family with two children, 12 and 8 years old: "Time and money are tight, but with both parents working full-time jobs, they feel they are providing for their families reasonably well" (p. 144)—but because the economic squeeze forces them both to work full time, they cannot control their children's access to the mass media, and they are afraid that their children are bombarded with sex and violence. Hewlett and West mention off-handedly that they have two televisions and are thinking of getting a third so that their children do not squabble about which programs to watch, they subscribe to cable TV and cannot keep track of what's on the 50 channels that their children can watch, their children can also go to the nearby mall to rent videos for their VCR, and they have several radio/cassette players in the house "with additional units in each of the family cars" (p. 144). They live in one of those post-Levittown suburbs that Hewlett and West like, but Hewlett and West have not thought about what an economic burden it is to support this style of housing and the multiple family cars that go with it. This is a fairly typical American family. Is their real problem that "money is tight"? Is the real solution to go back to the 1950s "American dream" of endlessly expanding suburban affluence?

69. You would think that liberals would have learned how much this sort of federal standard is worth from the failure of the Great Society housing programs of the 1960s. Lyndon Johnson's administration built high-rise housing projects in the slums of cities all over the country, all of which followed federal standards expressed as mathematical ratios of open space per resident, playground space per resident, floor space per resident, and so on. The standards were based on a long line of public health studies, going back to the studies of urban slums at the beginning of the twentieth century. Yet the housing projects proved to be even less livable than the slums they replaced: Studies comparing new housing projects with older neighborhoods across the street from them, both with the same socioeconomic profile, showed that crime rates were higher in the projects. Parents in some projects simply will not let their children go out of their apartments to play, because drug dealers have taken over the project grounds and sell drugs in the open space built according to federal standards, and HUD's HOPE VI program is demolishing projects and replacing them with something more like neighborhoods.

It should be obvious that this sort of federal standard can be useful only when purely technical questions are involved: The federal government can do a good job of setting safety standards that automobile manufacturers must follow, for example. But when it comes to human questions, such as the design of neighborhoods or the quality of child care, the most important issues cannot be reduced to the sort of quantitative standards that government bureaucracies formulate. How livable a neighborhood is does not depend on its open-space ratio nearly as much as it does on other, intangible factors. And how well children are raised does not depend on the number of square feet of floor space per child or on the number of college courses in developmental psychology that the child-care workers have taken nearly as much as it does on other, intangible factors.

The real problem with applying federal standards to this sort of human question is that the most important intangible factor that makes a neighborhood livable is people's feeling that it is *their* neighborhood, that they have a stake in it. Likewise, the most important intangible factor in raising children is the parents' feeling that it is their responsibility. When federal standards take people's neighborhoods or children away from them, the moral damage done is much more significant than any material benefits provided.

For the statistics showing higher crime rates in the projects than in older neighborhoods, see Oscar Newman, *Defensible Space: Crime Prevention Through Urban Design* (New York: Macmillan, 1972). Though there have been some criticisms of Newman's methodology, his conclusion that housing projects have higher crime rates is undoubtedly true and was widely recognized by the 1960s. The most famous discussion of the topic is in Jane Jacobs, *The Death and Life of Great American Cities* (New York: Vintage, 1961).

70. Hillary Clinton, *It Takes a Village: And Other Lessons Children Teach Us* (New York: Simon & Schuster, 1996), pp. 56–61.

71. John T. Bruer, *The Myth of the First Three Years: A New Understanding of Early Brain Development and Lifelong Learning* (New York: Free Press, 1999), p. 171.

72. Chapter 4 has a more detailed discussion of this issue.

73. "While Healthy Start operates on a consensual basis, states might also consider making public welfare or medical benefits contingent on agreement to allow home visits," Clinton, *It Takes a Village*, pp. 80–81.

74. *San Francisco Chronicle*, August 10, 1988, p. A2.

CHAPTER 3

75. Erik H. Erikson, *Childhood and Society* (New York: Norton, 1950), pp. 98–160.

76. Bruno Bettelheim, *The Children of the Dream* (New York: Avon, 1970), p. 16.

77. ". . . if we are to help the culturally deprived child—whether in city slums or impoverished rural areas—he had best be reared in an environment different from his home . . . ." Ibid., p. 18.

78. Ibid., p. 102.

79. Ibid., p. 137.

80. Ibid., pp. 137–138.

81. "If they are to make it successfully in their peer group, they must develop a high threshold against sensations, must screen out the finer nuances." Ibid., p. 139.

82. As Bettelheim says, adolescents on the kibbutz live "a group life that is devoid of true intimacy, though it remains intensely close." Ibid., p. 254.

83. "Kibbutz theory," Bettelheim says, "holds that his emotional needs are met mainly by his parents. And this radical separation between providing for his physical and emotional needs was meant to ensure that the pleasures of the latter would not be sullied by resented controls surrounding the first." Ibid., p. 87.

Bettelheim points out that the founders of the kibbutz movement misunderstood Freud's theories (though he does not admit how common similar ideas were among post-Freudians). Freud actually said, first, that the Oedipal situation is caused by deep attachment to parents, and, second, that all deep attachment is ambivalent. By trying to avoid all negative feelings, the kibbutz parents show "a fear of deep attachments pure and simple, of which ambivalence is a necessary part." Ibid., p. 51.

84. Ibid., pp. 203–204.

85. Ibid., p. 202.

86. As Bettelheim says, "A conscience based on 'obeying the rules of the game,' on a peer group 'morality of cooperation,' is highly concordant with what in psychoanalysis are described as the separate and different functions of the ego and superego. . . . This is quite different from a situation where obeying superego demands puts one at odds with the surrounding community." Ibid., p. 146.

87. "A personal stand was taken that went as much against the voice of the community as it forced the id and ego to get along with the superego. Luther's 'Here I stand. I cannot do otherwise' rightly heralds the Reformation in which the individual conscience was set against community mores. This highly individualized voice came from having internalized some very particular and highly personalized figures, chiefly the parents." Ibid., pp. 146–147.

88. Ibid., p. 285.

89. Ibid., p. 313.

90. Ibid., p. 223.

91. Ibid., p. 297.

92. "They neither hate them [their grandparents' ideals] nor make fun of them. . . . They feel nothing special about them, one way or the other. Kibbutz life, for this third generation, is not supposed to make this a better world, nor to prove anything. It is just the life they were born to and continue." Ibid., p. 289. This lack of idealism extends to other matters also. One of the founders, for example, who is a teacher of biology, says that his generation "had a real feeling for our animals because of our humanism" and had passionate arguments about ethical questions of how animals should be treated. By contrast, the kibbutz born "are only interested in the usefulness of the animal" and when ethical questions come up, "they have no feeling for our qualms. Their attitude is 'that's how things are.'" Ibid., p. 297.

93. Ibid., p. 298.

94. Ibid., p. 298.

95. Ibid., p. 339.

96. David Riesman, with Nathan Glazer and Reuel Denney, *The Lonely Crowd* (reprint, New Haven, Conn.: Yale University Press, 1969), pp. 9–11.

97. Ibid., p. 15.

98. Ibid., p. 21.

99. The "confident, secular man of the Renaissance" and the "God-fearing puritan," have very different ideals, Riesman notes, but "both these types are very much individuals, both are internally driven, and both are capable of pioneering." Ibid., pp. 40–41.

100. As Riesman puts it, inner-directed parents are concerned with their children's "characterological fitness and self-discipline." Ibid., p. 42.

101. "With the passing of the extended kinship family, the parent has his children much more under his own undivided and intensive scrutiny and control." Ibid.

102. "The conversation between parents and children, interrupted by the social distance that separates them, is continued by the child with himself in private." Ibid., p. 44.

103. Ibid.

104. Ibid., p. 47.

105. Ibid., p. 57.

106. "The teacher is supposed to see that the children learn a curriculum, not that they enjoy it or learn group cooperation." Ibid., p. 59.

107. Ibid., pp. 59–61.

108. With the decline of the intellectual focus of schooling, Riesman says, "the cooperation and leadership that are inculcated in and expected of the children are frequently contentless. In nursery school, it is not important whether Johnny plays with a truck or in the sandbox, but it matters very much whether he involves himself with Bill—via any object at all." Ibid., p. 63. Children no longer learn the lesson old-fashioned schools taught indirectly by emphasizing intellectual standards: that competence is what matters.

109. Ibid., p. 69.

110. Ibid., p. 70.

111. Ibid., p. 71.

112. "The function of the group is to have fun, to play; the deadly seriousness of the business, which might justify the child in making an issue of it, is therefore hidden." Ibid., p. 73.

113. Riesman welcomed the other-directed character because he contrasted it with the inner-directed character of the nineteenth century, when the inner-directed man turned into Babbitt. The first part of the book traces inner-direction to classical times and the Renaissance, but the second part of Riesman's book, which criticizes the inner-directed character, gets all its examples from nineteenth-century America. In fact, these two sections flatly contradict each other; for example, section one uses the Renaissance as an example of inner-direction (ibid., p. 40), but section two says that inner-direction did not emerge until after the Renaissance (ibid., 247).

Riesman also was too optimistic about the decline of inner-direction because he contrasted it with a strange new type of autonomy that he believed could emerge in the consumer society, which he discusses in the third section of his book. For example, he says, "recent movies can be interpreted as encouraging new styles in leisure and domesticity among men—with the implication that freedom from their peers will help them to increase their own competence as consumers and encourage their development toward autonomy." Ibid., p. 290. He even says we could teach children to be more autonomous by creating a "model consumer economy" and giving them scrip to spend, so that they could (as he puts it) learn to "express themselves through free consumer choice." Ibid., p. 302. This new idea of autonomy also makes Riesman say that traditional notions of marriage are "irrelevant to the greater demands [of] a leisure-oriented people. . . . What is obviously demanded is the development of a new model of marriage that finds its opportunity precisely in the choices that a free-divorce, leisure society opens up." Ibid., p. 281.

To understand why Riesman believed in this consumerist idea of autonomy, we must remember that he was writing at a time when the modern economy seemed omnipotent: Riesman emphasizes and reemphasizes that "the solution to the technical problems of production is in sight" (ibid., p. 263), so that the future must be devoted to consumption and leisure. (Apparently, the "technical problem" of raising children had also been solved, so Riesman could say that marriage should also become a form of leisure-oriented self-expression.) At the time, it was not realistic to challenge the consumer society in more fundamental ways, and Riesman's ideas about "autonomy" have to be read, in large part, as a counsel of despair.

114. He admitted in his introduction to the 1969 edition of his book that there is "in our high and popular culture a preference for anomie over adjustment, and more awareness of the anomie that does exist." Ibid., p. xv.

115. Other-directed parents still try to control their children, Riesman says; but because they can no longer hold up definitive standards for the children, they turn to psychological manipulation. This requires a new "lack of privacy" for the child, a breaking down of barriers of privacy that existed between inner-directed children and their parents (ibid., p. 52). In addition, other-directed parents worry not only about their child's character but also about their own relationship with the child; and so they are less likely to impose authoritative standards on the child and more likely to invent rationalizations and use them in a manipulative way to convince the child that certain behavior is right. "And when the child learns— this is part of his sensitive radar equipment—how to argue too," Riesman adds, "the parent is torn between giving in and falling uneasily back on the sterner methods of *his* inner-directed parents." Ibid., p. 53.

116. Lasch, *Haven*, p. xiv.

117. To be more precise, Lasch says the superego is transformed, "so that archaic, instinctual, death seeking elements increasingly predominate." Ibid., p. 123. In one major difference from Bettelheim, Lasch claims that the Oedipus complex described by Freud is universal. He says that the weakening of the family does not do away with infantile Oedipal fantasies: It makes it impossible for the child ever to get beyond them. Without the experience of being trained by the real father to soften them, the narcissist retains the infantile fantasy that authority is sinister and omnipotent. By contrast, Bettelheim observed a real weakening of the superego on the kibbutz.

In fact, Lasch himself seemed to believe that American children would eventually become more like children raised on the kibbutz: "Children do grow up in the kibbutz," he wrote, "and in fact develop into remarkably 'well-adjusted' adults: but it is precisely their 'adjustment,' their 'ability to work well with others,' their attachment to the peer group, their fear of being alone, . . . and their lack of introspection and of a highly developed inner life which may provide an ominous foretaste of our future." Ibid., p. 221 fn.

118. Ibid., p. 187.

119. Bettelheim, *Children of the Dream*, p. 128.

120. "The kibbutz child has little time or mental energy for thinking and feeling, particularly solitary thinking and feeling. For these he has virtually no chance, whereas many a middle-class child is alone to a degree that is just as unbalanced in the other direction." Ibid., pp. 140–141.

121. "Our middle-class children used to get more than their fill of being left alone in solitary play. . . . Lately, it must be said, their days have become so crowded that their chances for solitary activity have severely contracted." Ibid., p. 333.

122. Lasch, *Haven*, p. 188.

123. Lasch has said that the emergence of this manipulative, narcissistic character type, always on the look-out for its own advantage, proved that Riesman was wrong to believe that Americans were becoming more sociable and cooperative. Christopher Lasch, *The Culture of Narcissism: American Life in an Age of Diminishing Expectations* (New York: Norton, 1978b), p. 66. But actually Riesman made this error only in the later parts of *The Lonely Crowd*, where he was being overly optimistic about the future. In the first section, where he was discussing other-direction in historical context, he says very clearly that these "antagonistic cooperators" appeared because people who were economically ambitious needed to sell themselves on the personality market.

124. "Perhaps most important of all, there exist no delinquent peer groups, and all the peer associations that do exist exert control over possible delinquent tendencies." Bettelheim, *Children of the Dream*, p. 65. Bettelheim makes this same point at length on pp. 59–67 and 238 *et seq.*

125. In one recent case of senseless violence, three suburban teenagers in California drugged, murdered, and had sex with the dead body of a 15-year-old girl, because they thought it would help their death metal rock band make better music. This story was covered in California but did not get as much national attention as the teenagers who went "wilding" and brutally attacked a jogger in New York's Central Park a decade earlier—maybe because we are no longer as surprised by senseless violence. *San Francisco Chronicle*, March 8, 1997, p. A15.

126. "Attachment" theory was developed by John Bowlby and Mary Ainsworth during the 1950s and 1960s. Bowlby, impressed by studies on animals, theorized that children need a reliable attachment to a primary care giver, and he warned that children who were separated from their mothers had higher rates of physical and mental illness. See John Bowlby, *Maternal Care and Mental Health: A Report Prepared on behalf of the World Health Organization*, 2d ed. (Geneva: World Health Organization, 1952, originally published 1951).

During the 1960s, Mary Ainsworth did empirical studies of this issue. Researchers observed how 1-year-old infants behaved with their mothers, with a stranger, and alone. Ainsworth found that "securely attached" infants cried when their mothers left but were easily consoled when their mothers came back and were eager to explore the laboratory whenever their mothers were present;

"ambivalent" infants were clingy and afraid to explore the laboratory at first, became extremely agitated when their mothers left, and sought contact when their mothers returned; and "avoidant" infants kept their back turned to their mothers and explored the room, did not seem affected when the mother left, and avoided the mother when she returned. Through observations at home, Ainsworth found that the mothers of securely attached infants were responsive to their crying and feeding signals, while the mothers of the other children were either inconsistent or unresponsive. And her follow-up studies found that children who were not securely attached lacked self-reliance, were not enthusiastic about problem solving, and often became problem children with poor peer relations in school. See Mary D. Salter Ainsworth, et al., *Patterns of Attachment* (Hillsdale, N.J.: Erlbaum, 1977).

It took time for psychologists to recognize the importance of Ainsworth's work—she first published her results in 1969, but did not publish them in book form until 1977—but her work is now considered the foundation of "attachment theory," and the method of study that she used, called the Strange Situation, is a major empirical method that is now used for psychological research on infants.

The earliest studies of infants in day care, during the 1970s, had concluded that day care was just as good for children as family care. During the 1980s, though, researchers began doing studies of infants in day care using attachment theory and the Strange Situation, and they came up with very different conclusions. Jay Belsky, a psychologist at Pennsylvania State University, summarized this work and concluded that infants less than 1 year old who are in day care more than 20 hours a week tended to have the "avoidant" character that Ainsworth described. Belsky's findings are particularly compelling, since he had written in favor of day care during the 1970s, and a number of child psychiatrists said that their observations confirmed that full-time day care was bad for infants, although they had been afraid to admit it.

Belsky's claim that you should put infants under 1 year old in day care for no more than 20 hours a week provoked a storm of protest. The most prominent critic was Allison Clarke-Stewart, a psychologist at the University of California, Irvine, who argued that her studies showed smaller differences than Belsky's— 36 percent of the infants in day care insecurely attached, compared with 29 percent of those raised at home—and that this fact might not be significant, because the number of insecure infants in day care is similar to the normal range of insecure infants found in other countries.

Even more strikingly, Clarke-Stewart claims that Ainsworth's categories, based on observations of children raised at home, might not be appropriate for children raised in day care: They might not be "avoidant" but simply more independent than other children, more able to cope with strange situations because they are taken out of the home every day. Belsky admits that the Strange Situation might not be definitive and that other measurements should be developed, to see if they confirm its results.

The most remarkable thing about this dispute is how narrow its subject is. It is astounding that Clarke-Stewart and many other critics of Belsky claim that the

Strange Situation might not be appropriate for children raised in day care, because they might have a totally different sort of character than children raised at home, but that they refuse even to think about the moral or political meaning of this new type of character and that Belsky responds blandly by saying we need new measurements of psychological "adjustment." They refuse to discuss the most important issues, because there is no empirical technique available for studying them.

127. *San Francisco Chronicle*, April 4, 1997, p. A1.

CHAPTER 4

128. Benjamin Spock, quoted in the *San Francisco Chronicle*, May 3, 1990, p. B4.

129. Ibid.

130. Bettye M. Caldwell, "Infant Day Care—The Outcast Gains Respectability" in Pamela Roby ed., *Child Care—Who Cares: Foreign and Domestic Infant and Early Childhood Development Policies* (New York: Basic Books, 1973), p. 21.

131. John L. Kramer, Thomas R. Pope, and Lawrence C. Phillips, *Federal Taxation: 1997* (Upper Saddle River, N.J.: Prentice Hall, 1996), pp. 14–15.

132. An estimate by the Urban Institute, cited in the *San Francisco Chronicle*, February 8, 1989, p. C5.

133. Families in which the wife does not work have a median income of $28,779, while families with two full-time wage earners have a median income of $56,078 (Census, *Statistical Abstract, 1996*, p. 471). Since women earn less than men, the husbands in the two-income families must earn more than the husbands in the single-income family. Apart from the wife's income, men in dual-income families generally have better-paying jobs than men in single-income families.

134. *New York Times*, December 25, 1996, p. C2.

135. *New York Times*, October 22, 1999, p. A16.

136. The median income of all year-round, full-time female workers in 1994 was $23,265 (Census, *Statistical Abstract, 1996*, p. 469). We can use the proportion of income that all Americans pay in taxes to come up with a rough calculation of after-tax income. In 1995, total personal income was $6,101.7 billion, and total personal payments for taxes and social insurance was $1088.8 billion, 17.8 percent of personal income (Census, *Statistical Abstract, 1996*, p. 451). This would take over $4,150 out of the median income of a full-time working woman, leaving after-tax income below $20,000.

137. Hewlett and West, *War Against Parents*, p. 250.

138. From their Web site, http://www.kindercare.com.

139. By contrast, during 1995, use of day care overall increased by 5 percent: on-site corporate day care is growing five times as rapidly as the industry as a whole. *San Francisco Chronicle*, December 23, 1996, p. A3.

140. Ibid.

141. To do this, employers establish Dependent Care Assistance Plans, deduct up to $5,000 per year from an employee's regular paycheck to put in this

plan, and use this money to reimburse the employee when they are presented with receipts for child-care expenses; the income paid into this plan is tax-free.

142. Unfortunately, the final findings of this study were not published before this book went to press, though some were reported in the news media. This data (and the quoted headline) are from the *New York Times*, October 22, 1999, p. A16.

143. Bruer, *Myth of the First Three Years*, p. 191. This book is the best account of how day-care advocates have misinterpreted brain science, and it is the basis of most of this section.

144. "When these [socioeconomic] factors are statistically controlled, however, it appears that differences between schools account for only a small fraction of differences in pupil achievement." James S. Coleman, et al., *Equality of Educational Opportunity* (Washington, D.C.: U.S. Government Printing Office, 1966), pp. 21–22.

145. "The effect of schooling varies among different groups and is greater for minorities, except for Asians, than for whites: for example, quality of schooling accounts for 10 percent of the difference in achievement among southern whites and 20 percent among southern blacks." Ibid., p. 22. Though Coleman does not make this point, it is evident that school has the least influence and the family has the most influence among the groups that are the most successful: Asians, the most successful minority group, are the minority group for whom schooling influences achievement least. In seems that schooling has more influence among less successful groups not because the schools help them more but because their families and communities are contributing less.

146. James Coleman, "Effects of School on Learning: The IEA Findings," paper presented at Conference on Educational Achievement, Harvard University, November 1973, p. 40, cited in Hewlett and West, *War Against Parents*, p. 50.

147. Christopher Jencks, et al., *Inequality: A Reassessment of the Effect of Family and Schooling in America* (New York: Basic Books, 1972), p. 39.

148. Ibid., pp. 158–159.

149. A comprehensive review of the literature by Eric Hanushek of the University of Rochester has shown that there is no correlation between achievement and class size, teacher credentials, or the amount of money spent on schooling. After looking at the 187 studies that considered the effect of spending on educational performance, Hanushek concluded that "there is no strong or systematic relationship between school expenditures and student performance" (p. 47). For example, of the 152 studies that considered the effect of class size on achievement, 125 did not show statistically significant differences in achievement in classes of different sizes, 14 showed higher achievement in the smaller classes, and 13 showed higher achievement in the larger classes. Results were similar in studies of increased expenditures on teacher salaries, facilities, and administration. However, Hanushek adds that studies have shown that "teachers and schools differ dramatically in their effectiveness" and that the Coleman Report was wrong in concluding that quality of schooling has little or no effect on achievement: It is only the easily measurable components of school quality—such as spending per

student and teacher–student ratio—that have no effect. Eric A. Hanushek, "The Impact of Differential Expenditures on School Performance," *Educational Researcher*, May 1989, pp. 45–50.

The one important study with contrary results, which is constantly cited by progressives demanding smaller class size, is the Tennessee class-size study, which found that there is a lasting improvement in achievement if kindergarten through third-grade classes have 13 to 17 pupils, one-third fewer than the ordinary classes used in the control group. Critics of this study have pointed out that the smaller classes had proportionally fewer minority students, so that pupils might not really have been assigned randomly to the smaller classes and to the control group, and many people associated with the study believe that this benefit is a "start-up effect," that is, the smaller class sizes made it easier for children to adjust to starting school but would not improve achievement in higher grades. Most important, the fact that students knew whether they were in the experimental group or the control group makes it likely that the improvement was a placebo effect; people always tout this as a controlled experiment, but it was not at all like a real double-blind controlled scientific experiment.

In fact, there is now evidence that the improvements in the Tennessee class-size study were almost exclusively the result of a placebo effect. On the basis of the Tennessee findings, California spent $3.7 billion to reduce class size, cutting average class size from 30 to 20 students for grades K–3. The preliminary evaluation of smaller classes found that, after 3 years, reading, math and language scores of third-graders improved only 2 to 3 points on 1998 achievement tests—much, much less than the improvement in Tennessee. *San Francisco Chronicle*, June 23, 1999, p. 1. This small improvement also might have been the result of a placebo effect, since the teachers, parents, and students expected the smaller classes to improve performance; we would expect some placebo effect for this sort of statewide experiment, but a much smaller one than in the controlled experiment in Tennessee, where all the students were subject to intense scrutiny and high expectations.

For more information on the Tennessee class-size study, see Frederick Mosteller, "The Tennessee Study of Class Size in the Early School Grades," *The Future of Children* 5, no. 2 (Summer/Fall 1995): 113–127.

150. Spending per pupil in average daily attendance was $2,803 in 1963–1964 and $4,965 in 1979–1980 (both figures in 1995–1996 dollars). U.S. Department of Education, National Center for Education Statistics, *Digest of Education Statistics 1996*, NCES 96-133 (Washington, D.C., 1996). The pupil–teacher ratio also declined dramatically, from 29.4 in 1960 to 20.1 in 1980. *Digest of Education Statistics 1996*, p. 74. Yet SAT scores declined from an averaged combined math–verbal score of 980 in 1963–1964 to 890 in 1979–1980. *Digest of Education Statistics 1996*, p. 127.

151. The National Commission on Excellence in Education, *A Nation at Risk: The Imperative for Educational Reform* (Washington, D.C.: U.S. Government Printing Office, 1983), p. 11.

152. Carnegie Foundation for the Advancement of Teaching, *Report Card on School Reform: The Teachers Speak* (Princeton, N.J.: Author, 1988).

153. Cited in *San Francisco Chronicle*, December 12, 1988, p. A8.

154. Lawrence Steinberg, *Beyond the Classroom: Why School Reform Has Failed and What Parents Need to Do* (New York: Simon & Schuster, 1996), pp. 118–119.

155. Cited in *New York Times*, August 7, 1997, p. A12.

156. Steinberg, *Beyond the Classroom*, pp. 120–121.

157. "Over Million Students Apply for $170 Million in Scholarships Offered by Financier," *New York Times*, April 21, 1999, p. A25.

158. John O. Norquist, *The Wealth of Cities: Revitalizing the Centers of American Life* (Reading, Mass.: Addison-Wesley, 1998), p. 88.

159. "Study Shows Voucher Pupils Thriving in Private Schools," *New York Times*, August 13, 1996, p. A6. There was extensive press coverage of the first study of the program, by University of Wisconsin professor John Witte, which found that these students' academic performance was no better than public school students', but critics pointed out that this study did not correct for parental education, occupation, welfare dependence, whether the house is headed by one parent or two, the students' native language, and other important variables.

160. Norquist, *Wealth of Cities*, p. 86.

161. *San Francisco Chronicle*, September 13, 1999, p. A4.

162. "25% of Kids Already Attend 'Alternative' Schools, Study Finds," *San Francisco Chronicle*, September 8, 1999, p. A10.

163. In 1960, only 27.6 percent of married women with children under 17 years old worked. The stay-at-home mother was still typical. Census, *Statistical Abstract, 1996*, p. 400.

164. The Family and Medical Leave Act of 1993 allows up to 12 weeks of leave, but this law only applies to companies with more than 50 employees, so it does not cover more than 40 percent of private-sector employees.

165. "Redrawing the American Gothic," *New Perspectives Quarterly* 7, no. 1 (Winter 1990): 23.

166. Schor, *Overworked American*, p. 133.

167. One survey of male heads of households found that 85 percent said they had no choice of work hours. Another survey of married men found that 85 percent had to work hours they would not choose in order to keep their jobs. Ibid., p. 128.

168. Hewlett and West, *War Against Parents*, p. 234.

169. *San Francisco Chronicle*, June 1, 1989, p. A6.

170. Felice Schwartz, "Careerus Interruptus," *New Perspectives Quarterly* 7, no. 1 (Winter 1990): p. 17.

171. Hewlett and West, *War Against Parents*, p. 234.

172. *New York Times*, September 1, 1997, p. B7.

173. *San Francisco Chronicle*, March 14, 1989, p. B3.

174. For a thorough discussion of this issue, see C. Eugene Steuerle, "Valuing Marital Commitment: The Radical Restructuring of Our Tax and Transfer Systems," *The Responsive Community* 2, no. 9 (Spring 1999): 35–45. Also available from the Urban Institute.

175. Pretax child poverty rates are 21 percent in France, 26 percent in Britain, and 22 percent in the United States; and child poverty rates after tax and trans-

fer are 4 percent in France, 8 percent in Britain, and 20 percent in the United States. Hewlett and West, *War Against Parents*, p. 122.

176. William A. Galston, "Needed: A Not-So-Fast Divorce Law," *New York Times*, December 27, 1995, p. A11.

CHAPTER 5

177. Ellen Convisser, president of the National Organization for Women's Boston Chapter, cited in *San Francisco Chronicle*, July 1, 1989.

178. Sar A. Levitan, Richard S. Belous, and Frank Gallo, *What's Happening to the American Family? Tensions, Hopes, Realities*, rev. ed. (Baltimore: Johns Hopkins University Press, 1998), p. 85.

179. In constant 1958 dollars, per-capita GNP in 1890 was $836 and per- capita GNP in 1970 was $3,555. Census, *Historical Statistics of the United States*, p. 224. In constant 1992 dollars, per-capita GNP was $16,520 in 1970 and $25,615 in 1995. Census, *Statistical Abstract, 1996*, p. 448. In total, then, real, per-capita GNP was more than 6.5 times as high in 1995 as in 1890.

180. William R. Mattox, Jr., "The Parent Trap," *Policy Review* 55 (Winter 1991): 6.

181. *Money*, July 1988, p. 70.

182. Ibid., p. 73.

183. For example, a survey of 5,000 eighth-grade children in southern California found that the more hours the children were left by themselves after school, the greater the risk of substance abuse (overall, these children were twice as likely to drink alcohol and take drugs); the correlation held regardless of the child's race, sex, or economic status. Another study by Dr. Michael D. Resnick, which surveyed 90,000 teenagers, the largest sampling ever done, found that children are more likely to attempt suicide, be violent, or use drugs if they have no close connection to their parents, and that the presence of a parent at home after school, at dinner, and at bedtime is enough to reduce this behavior. West and Hewlett, *War Against Parents*, p. 49.

184. Ibid.

185. Borsodi explained this by saying that the efficiencies of large-scale production can be outweighed by higher distribution costs. Large-scale manufacturing requires extra spending on wholesaling, retailing, and transportation of the raw materials and finished products, and Borsodi claimed that these extra costs outweigh the efficiencies of mass production for most nondurable goods, such as food. See, for example, Ralph Borsodi, *The Distribution Age* (New York: D. Appleton & Co., 1927). Borsodi did experiments in his own homestead, using the most efficient small machinery available and figuring the cost of his own labor at market value, to compare the cost of producing and buying foods such as canned tomatoes. Ralph Borsodi, *Flight from the City* (Suffern, N.Y.: School of Living, 1947), pp. 11–12.

186. Scott Burns, *The Household Economy: Its Shape, Origins, and Future* (Boston: Beacon, 1975), p. 42.

187. Joe Dominguez and Vicki Robin, *Your Money or Your Life* (New York: Penguin USA, 1993).

188. Robert Gilman, "A Movement Blossoms: After a Fling with Overconsumption in the '80s, Many Are Turning to Frugality in Its Fullest Meaning," an interview with Joe Dominguez and Vicki Robin, *In Context*, Winter 1993–1994, p. 23.

189. *Money*, July 1988, p. 96.

190. *Better Homes and Gardens*, October 1987, p. 36.

191. Census, *Statistical Abstract, 1996*.

192. Sinclair Lewis, *Babbitt* (reprint, New York: Signet, 1961), p. 149.

193. Michael Renner, *Rethinking the Role of the Automobile*, Worldwatch Paper No. 84 (Washington, D.C.: Worldwatch Institute, 1988), p. 46. A number of studies have shown that the average American's travel time has remained constant since the 1840s, despite all the changes in transportation technology since that time. Higher speeds have not made it more convenient to get around; they have changed living patterns so that people travel longer distances. Through the streetcar suburbs, new transportation technology and the living patterns that went with them made cities more livable; but more recently, they have made cities less livable. See Charles Siegel, *Slow Is Beautiful: Speed Limits as Decisions on Urban Form* (Berkeley, CA: Preservation Institute, 1997).

194. The typical American house was 750 square feet in 1950 and 2000 square feet in 1989. Schor, *Overworked American*, p. 111.

195. For an overview of this movement, see Peter Katz, *The New Urbanism: Toward an Architecture of Community* (New York: McGraw-Hill, 1994).

196. ERE Yarmouth and Real Estate Research Corporation (RERC), *Emerging Trends in Real Estate, 1998* (Chicago: Real Estate Research Corporation, 1997), p. 24.

197. *Wall Street Journal*, December 26, 1995, p. 1.

198. The most detailed cost comparison is in a study done at the University of British Columbia. The study compared three possible neighborhood patterns: a "status-quo" suburban pattern, a "traditional" pattern, and a traditional pattern with an ecological element designed to preserve natural systems on a site. Then it did two detailed designs for 14-acre parcels in a Vancouver suburb, one in the status quo pattern and the other in the traditional pattern with ecological underlay. It found that the cost of land was $51,467 per unit for the status quo design and $11,346 per unit for the sustainable design, and the cost of site infrastructure was $15,758 per unit for the status quo design and $2,953 per unit for the sustainable design. Total cost per dwelling unit was $159,687 per unit for the status quo design and $98,719 per unit for the sustainable design. However, the status quo design had average units of 2,300 square feet and the sustainable design had a slightly smaller average unit of 2,090 square feet. After correcting for the difference in size, the cost of a unit in the sustainable design is just slightly over 68 percent of the cost in the status quo design. (All these costs have been converted to American dollars.) Patrick Condon, "Alternative Development Standards for Sustainable Communities" (April 1998), James Taylor Chair in Landscape and Livable Environments, Landscape Architecture Program, 6368 Stores Road, University of British Columbia, Vancouver, British Columbia.

199. Peter Calthorpe, *The Next American Metropolis: Ecology, Community, and the American Dream* (New York: Princeton Architectural Press, 1993), pp. 35, 48.

200. See Patrick Hare, "One-Car Mortgages and One-Car Rents: Making Housing Affordable by Reducing Second Car Ownership," *Land Development*, Spring–Summer 1994, pp. 12–14.

201. Herbert J. Gans, *The Levittowners: Ways of Life and Politics in a New Suburban Community* (New York: Pantheon, 1967).

202. See Mary C. Howell, *Helping Ourselves: Women and the Human Network* (Boston: Beacon 1975), esp. pp. 70–94.

203. In Ithaca, New York, a community group called the Barter Bank of Ithaca has printed and distributed "Ithaca Hours," which are the size of dollar bills and can be redeemed either for 1 hour of labor or for $10 (the average hourly wage in the area). The Barter Bank publishes a monthly newsletter, where hundreds of people list services that they will trade for Ithaca Hours, and some local businesses also accept Hours instead of cash. For a how-to book on setting up this sort of local barter-currency, see Edgar Cahn and Jonathan Rowe, *Time Dollars: The New Currency That Enables Americans to Turn Their Hidden Resource — Time — into Personal Security and Community Renewal* (Emmaus, Pa.: Rodale Press, 1992).

204. Christopher Lasch, *Women and the Common Life: Love, Marriage, and Feminism*, ed. Elizabeth Lasch-Quinn (New York: Norton, 1997), pp. 95–100.

205. Robert D. Putnam, "Bowling Alone: America's Declining Social Capital," *Journal of Democracy*, January 1995, pp. 65–78, and "The Strange Disappearance of Civic America," *The American Prospect*, Winter 1996, pp. 34–48.

206. Data are taken from U.S. Department of Commerce and U.S. Bureau of the Census, *Long-Term Economic Growth: 1860–1965* (Washington, D.C.: U.S. Government Printing Office, 1966) and from U.S. Bureau of Economic Statistics, *The Handbook of Basic Economic Statistics* (Washington, D.C.: 1976).

207. John Maynard Keynes, *Essays in Persuasion* (New York: Harcourt, Brace & Co., 1932), p. 365.

208. Ibid., p. 367.

209. See Benjamin Kline Hunnicutt, *Work Without End: Abandoning Shorter Hours for the Right to Work* (Philadelphia: Temple University Press, 1988). The history that follows is based on this book.

210. Both editorials cited in Robert S. Lynd and Helen M. Lynd, *Middletown: A Study in American Culture* (London: Constable & Co., 1929), p. 88.

211. Benjamin Hunnicutt, "The Pursuit of Happiness: A Six-Hour Day at the Kellogg Company Plant Liberated Time for Family and Community and Provided Jobs for the Unemployed," *In Context*, Winter 1993–1994, pp. 34–38.

212. Packard, *Waste Makers*, p. 17.

213. Schor, *Overworked American*, p. 36.

214. According to a study by the International Labor Organization, American workers put in an average of 1,966 hours at work in 1997, nearly 4 percent more than the 1,883 recorded in 1980. By contrast, the Japanese work 1,889, the French work 1,656, and the Germans work 1,560 hours per year. "Americans Lead the Way in Hours Worked," *New York Times*, September 7, 1999, p. C9.

215. Per-capita GNP in constant 1992 dollars was $18,572 in 1973 and $25,588 in 1995, an increase of over 37 percent. Per-capita personal consumption expenditures in constant 1992 dollars were $11,950 in 1973 and $17,403 in 1995, an increase of over 45 percent. Census, *Statistical Abstract, 1996*, p. 448.

216. Rudd Lubbers, "The Dutch Way," *New Perspectives Quarterly*, Fall 1997, p. 15.

217. *San Francisco Chronicle*, November 9, 1999, p. A14.

218. See Chapter 1, note 9.

219. These indexes are all based on the idea that the GDP measures total economic activity but does not measure the net benefit people get from that activity. For example, if a factory produces $100 million worth of products, and its emissions cause cancer cases that cost $10 million to treat, it adds $110 million to the GDP—$10 million more it would have if it had made the products without causing cancer. To come up with a measure of actual well-being, these studies subtract what economists call "defensive expenditures" from the GDP—expenditures that are only necessary to deal with problems caused by growth. They also try to calculate imputed costs of air pollution, noise, resource depletion, and other environmental costs of growth that are left out of the GDP entirely, and they try to correct for the declining productive role of the home and community as the money economy takes over most of their functions.

220. Clifford Cobb, Gary Sue Goodman, and Mathis Wackernagel, *Why Bigger Isn't Better: The Genuine Progress Indicator—1999 Update* (San Francisco: Redefining Progress, 1999), pp. 11–12. See also Clifford Cobb, Ted Halstead, and Jonathan Rowe, "If the GDP Is Up, Why Is America Down?" *Atlantic Monthly*, October 1995, pp. 57–78, for a general discussion of their conclusions. A similar study is the Daly–Cobb Index of Sustainable Economic Welfare, which shows that economic well-being increased substantially during the 1950s and 1960s, leveled off from 1968 until the end of the 1970s, and began to decline during the 1980s. Herman E. Daly and John B. Cobb, Jr., *For the Common Good: Redirecting the Economy Toward Community, the Environment, and a Sustainable Future* (Boston: Beacon, 1989), pp. 401–455.

CHAPTER 6

221. Levitan et al., *What's Happening*, p. 131.

222. Engels's book synthesized the work of the German scholar Johann Jakob Bachofen, whose 1861 book *Mother Right* had analyzed classical mythology and shown that the patriarchal classical period was preceded by a matriarchal period, with the work of the American anthropologist Lewis Henry Morgan, whose studies of the Iroquois Indians had shown that their societies were still organized according to matrilineal descent. Friedrich Engels, "Origin of the Family, Private Property, and the State," in Karl Marx and Friedrich Engels, *Selected Works* (New York: International Publishers, 1974, originally published 1884), p. 522.

223. In Engels's bombastic prose, "the woman was degraded, enthralled, the slave of the man's lust, a mere instrument for breeding children. . . . In order to

guarantee the fidelity of the wife, that is, the paternity of the children, the woman is placed in the man's absolute power; if he kills her, he is but exercising his right." Ibid., pp. 496–497.

224. Ibid., p. 511.

225. "The impending social revolution . . . by transforming at least the far greater part of permanent inheritable wealth—the means of production—into social property, will reduce all this anxiety about inheritance to a minimum." Ibid., p. 511.

226. "The duration of the urge of individual sex love differs very much according to the individual, particularly among men; and a definite cessation of affection, or its displacement by a new passionate love, makes separation a blessing. . . . People will only be spared the experience of wading through the useless mire of divorce proceedings." Ibid., p. 517.

227. Ibid., p. 511.

228. Bronislaw Malinowski, *Argonauts of the Western Pacific: An Account of Native Enterprise and Adventure in the Archipelagoes of Melanesian New Guinea* (New York: Dutton, 1960, originally published 1922).

229. Margaret Mead, *Coming of Age in Samoa* (New York: William Morrow, 1961, originally published 1928), p. 200. In another book, Mead writes about adolescence: "From the conflict between those who have mastered the culture and those who have yet to master it, there comes a kind of strain which seems . . . inevitable. Only if a culture lacks intensity in every respect, as does Samoa, can this strain be eliminated." Margaret Mead, *From the South Seas: Studies of Adolescence and Sex in Primitive Societies* (New York: William Morrow, 1939), p. 219.

230. Mead, *Coming of Age*, p. 98.

231. "Premarital affairs and extramarital affairs were conducted with enough lightness not to threaten the reliable sex relationships between married couples." Margaret Mead, *Male and Female: A Study of the Sexes in a Changing World* (New York: William Morrow, 1949), p. 114.

232. Ibid., p. 114.

233. In Samoa, "the child owes no emotional allegiance to its father and mother. These personalities are merged in a large household group of fostering adults. The child unfettered by emotional ties finds sufficient satisfaction in the mild warmth" of the group. Mead, *From the South Seas*, p. 239.

234. A Samoan child "is fed when he is hungry, carried when he is tired, allowed to sleep when he wills. If he does wrong—cries and disturbs the dignity of some consultation going on among the elders, defecates in the house, or has a temper tantrum—it is not he who is punished, but the child-nurse whose duty it is to keep him out of such difficulties and to lug him out of earshot when he cries. Children are too young to know how to behave, but they may be trusted to develop sense—*mafaufau*—in time." Mead, *Male and Female*, p. 114.

235. "For sixteen or seventeen years, the principal determinant of a young Samoan's behavior has been the standard of his age group, not the personality of any adult. So strong is the tradition of conformity to the age standard, that . . . Samoan men are very much alike when compared with Manus men." Mead, *From the South Seas*, pp. 232–233.

236. Mead, *Coming of Age*, p. 200.

237. Ibid., p. 207.

238. Derek Freeman, *Margaret Mead and Samoa: The Making and Unmaking of an Anthropological Myth* (Cambridge, Mass.: Harvard University Press, 1983). Freeman's study has been controversial, but it has shaken anthropologists' faith in Mead's work. For a summary of the controversy, see Conrad Phillip Kottak, *Cultural Anthropology*, 6th ed. (New York: McGraw-Hill, 1994), pp. 286–287.

239. Freeman, *Margaret Mead*, p. 290.

240. Erich Fromm, *The Sane Society* (New York: Fawcett World Library, 1968) is a complete formulation of these ideas, which are also present in many other books by Fromm.

241. Byron, *Manfred* (1817), Act I, Scene 2, line 48.

242. The most famous statement of this theme is Ferdinand Tönnies, *Gemeinschaft und Gesellschaft* (New York: Harper & Row, 1963, originally published 1887). These terms are difficult to translate, but *Gemeinschaft* refers to a social order that is held together by organic bonds, such as shared beliefs, and *Gesellschaft* refers to a social order held together by more mechanical, external bonds, such as economic interest.

243. Engels's criticism of nineteenth-century bourgeois marriages that were based on calculations about property and social position is even more out of date. How many of us today know a father who arranged his daughter's marriage in order to advance himself in "society"?

244. Aldous Huxley, *Brave New World* (New York: Bantam Books, 1953, originally published 1932), pp. 25–26.

245. Ibid., p. 27. Likewise, they describe the family as "home—a few small rooms, stiflingly over-inhabited by a man, by a periodically teeming woman, by a rabble of boys and girls . . . Psychically, it was . . . reeking with emotion. What suffocating intimacies, what dangerous, insane, obscene relationships between the members of the family group!" Ibid., p. 24.

246. Ibid., p. 160.

247. Ibid., p. 155.

248. See *Plain* magazine, number 12, April 1996, special issue on The Second Luddite Congress.

249. Marilyn Waring, *If Women Counted: A New Feminist Economics* (New York: Harper & Row, 1988).

250. Barbara Brandt, *Whole Life Economics: Revaluing Daily Life* (Philadelphia: New Society Publishers, 1995), pp. 51–56 and throughout.

251. See Waring, *If Women Counted*, pp. 300–301.

252. Cited in Christopher Hill, *The Century of Revolution: 1603–1714* (New York: Norton, 1980), p. 259.

253. See Lasch, *Women and the Common Life*, pp. 118–119.

254. Clinton, *It Takes a Village*, p. 13.

255. Incidentally, Hillary Clinton herself lives in a neighborhood where there are no sidewalks, so it is not surprising that she does not see any neighbors walking by. During her senatorial campaign, after she attacked Rudolph Giuliani for having the police move on homeless people who sit on the sidewalks in New York

City, a *New York Times* reporter dressed as a homeless person and went to her neighborhood in Chappaqua to see how the police there would treat people who sit on the sidewalk, but he found: "I couldn't legally sit down anywhere near her home. There were no sidewalks on her cul de sac or on nearby roads." John Tierney, "Metropolis or Village, Don't Sleep on the Street," *New York Times*, December 15, 1999, p. A23.

256. In September 1999, there was a poll of 500 French workers in companies that had reduced the workweek to 35 hours (as required by recent legislation in that country), asking what they did with their free time. The answers with the highest responses were:

1. Spend more time with family and children: 71% of men, 66% of women
2. Take more time for daily tasks: 29% of men, 62% of women
3. Do odd jobs (*bricoler*) and garden: 53% of men, 25% of women
4. Do sports, cultural, or artistic activities: 48% of men, 29% of women
5. Rest more: 24% of men, 48% of women
6. Spend more time with friends and acquaintances: men, 31%; women, 34%

People make good use of the extra time. Only 1% of both men and women said they did nothing in particular with the time.

There are important gender differences. Women put more emphasis on taking time for daily tasks and resting, which shows they are more overworked than men now, because they have jobs and a "second shift" of work at home.

There are also important class differences. Managers were more likely to spend time on cultural or artistic activities (58%), while manual workers were more likely to spend time on gardening and *bricolage*, which could mean do-it-yourself projects as well as odd jobs (60%). (Source: *Libération*, October 5, 1999.) In this example of a working-class family, the man spends his free time on what the French would call *bricolage*.

BIBLIOGRAPHY

Ainsworth, Mary D. Salter, et al. (1977). *Patterns of attachment*. Hillsdale, NJ: Erlbaum.

Ariès, Philippe. (1962). *Centuries of childhood: A social history of family life*, trans. Robert Baldick. New York: Vintage.

Bellah, Robert, Madsen, Richard, Sullivan, William, Swidler, Ann, and Tipton, Steven. (1985). *Habits of the heart: Individualism and commitment in American life*. New York: Harper & Row.

Bellamy, Edward. (1888). *Looking backward, 2000–1887*. Boston: Ticknor & Company.

Bettelheim, Bruno. (1970). *The children of the dream*. New York: Avon.

Blankenhorn, David. (1995). *Fatherless America: Confronting our most urgent social problem*. New York: Basic Books.

Borsodi, Ralph. (1927). *The distribution age*. New York: D. Appleton & Co.

Borsodi, Ralph. (1947). *Flight from the city*. Suffern, NY: School of Living.

Bowlby, John. (1952). *Maternal care and mental health: A report prepared on behalf of the World Health Organization*, 2d ed. Geneva: World Health Organization. (Original work published 1951)

Brandt, Barbara. (1995). *Whole life economics: Revaluing daily life*. Philadelphia: New Society Publishers.

Bruer, John T. (1999). *The myth of the first three years: A new understanding of early brain development and lifelong learning*. New York: Free Press.

Burns, Scott. (1975). *The household economy: Its shape, origins, and future*. Boston: Beacon.

Cahn, Edgar, and Rowe, Jonathan. (1992). *Time dollars: The new currency that enables Americans to turn their hidden resource — time — into personal security and community renewal*. Emmaus, PA: Rodale Press.

Caldwell, Bettye M. (1973). Infant day care—the outcast gains respectability. In Pamela Roby (Ed.), *Child care—who cares: Foreign and domestic infant and early childhood development policies*. New York: Basic Books.

Calthorpe, Peter. (1993). *The next American metropolis: Ecology, community, and the American dream*. New York: Princeton Architectural Press.

Carnegie Foundation for the Advancement of Teaching. (1988). *Report card on school reform: The teachers speak*. Princeton, NJ: Author.

Clinton, Hillary. (1996). *It takes a village: And other lessons children teach us*. New York: Simon & Schuster.

Cobb, Clifford, Goodman, Gary Sue, and Wackernagel, Mathis. (1999). *Why bigger isn't better: The genuine progress indicator—1999 update*. San Francisco: Redefining Progress.

Cobb, Clifford, Halstead, Ted, and Rowe, Jonathan. (1995, October). "If the GDP is up, why is America down?" *Atlantic Monthly*, pp. 57–78.

Coleman, James S., et al. (1966). *Equality of educational opportunity*. Washington, DC: U.S. Government Printing Office.

Condon, Patrick. (1998, April). Alternative development standards for sustainable communities. James Taylor Chair in Landscape and Livable Environments, Landscape Architecture Program, 6368 Stores Road, University of British Columbia, Vancouver, British Columbia.

Coons, John E., and Sugarman, Stephen D. (1971). *Family choice in education: A model state system for vouchers*. Berkeley: University of California at Berkeley Institute of Governmental Studies.

Coontz, Stephanie. (1992). *The way we never were: American families and the nostalgia trap*. New York: Basic Books.

Coontz, Stephanie. (1997). *The way we really are: Coming to terms with America's changing families*. New York: Basic Books.

Daly, Herman E., and Cobb, John B., Jr. (1989). *For the common good: Redirecting the economy toward community, the environment, and a sustainable future*. Boston: Beacon.

Dominguez, Joe, and Robin, Vicki. (1993). *Your money or your life*. New York: Penguin USA.

Engels, Frederick. (1974). Origin of the family, private property and the state. In Karl Marx and Frederick Engels, *Selected works*. New York: International Publishers. (Original work published 1884)

ERE Yarmouth and Real Estate Research Corporation. (1997). *Emerging trends in real estate, 1998*. Chicago: Real Estate Research Corporation (RERC).

Erikson, Erik H. (1950). *Childhood and society*. New York: Norton.

Etzioni, Amitai. (1993). *The spirit of community: Rights responsibilities, and the communitarian agenda*. New York: Crown.

Freeman, Derek. (1983). *Margaret Mead and Samoa: The making and unmaking of an anthropological myth*. Cambridge, MA: Harvard University Press.

Friedan, Betty. (1977). *The feminine mystique*. New York: Dell. (Original work published 1963)

Fromm, Erich. (1968). *The sane society*. New York: Fawcett World Library.

Frost, J. William. (1973). *The Quaker family*. New York: St. Martin's Press.

Galbraith, John Kenneth. (1958). *The affluent society*. Boston: Houghton Mifflin.

Gans, Herbert J. (1967). *The Levittowners: Ways of life and politics in a new suburban community*. New York: Pantheon.

Gilder, George. (1973). *Sexual suicide*. New York: Quadrangle.

Gilder, George. (1974). *Naked nomads: Unmarried men in America*. New York: Quadrangle/New York Times Books.

Gilder, George. (1981). *Wealth and poverty*. New York: Basic Books.

Gilder, George. (1986). *Men and marriage*. New York: Pelican Publishing.

Gilman, Charlotte Perkins. (1989). *The yellow wallpaper and other writings*. New York: Bantam Books.

Gilman, Robert. (1993–1994, Winter). A movement blossoms: After a fling with overconsumption in the '80s, many are turning to frugality in its fullest meaning (an interview with Joe Dominguez and Vicki Robin). *In Context*, pp. 23–26.

Greenleaf, Barbara Kaye. (1978). *Children through the ages: A history of childhood*. New York: Barnes & Noble.

Hagar, Laura. (1997, February 21). The American family is dead! Long live American families (an interview with Judith Stacey). *The Express* (San Francisco), pp. 1, 6–13.

Hansen, Mark, and Huang, Yuanlin. (1997, March). Road supply and traffic in California urban areas. *Transportation Research A, 31* (3), 205–218.

Hanushek, Eric A. (1989, May). The impact of differential expenditures on school performance. *Educational Researcher*, pp. 45–50.

Hare, Patrick. (1994, Spring–Summer). One-car mortgages and one-car rents: Making housing affordable by reducing second car ownership. *Land Development, 7* (1), 12–14.

Hayden, Dolores. (1981). *The grand domestic revolution: A history of feminist designs for American homes, neighborhoods, and cities*. Cambridge, MA: MIT Press.

Henderson, David R. (1989, July). *Child care tax credits: A supply-side success story*. National Center for Policy Analysis Policy Report No. 140.

Hewlett, Sylvia Ann. (1990, Winter). The feminization of the work force. *New Perspectives Quarterly, 7* (1), 13–15.

Hewlett, Sylvia Ann, and West, Cornel. (1998). *The war against parents*. Boston: Houghton Mifflin.

Hill, Christopher. (1980). *The century of revolution: 1603–1714*. New York: Norton.

Himmelfarb, Gertrude. (1996). *The demoralization of society: From Victorian virtues to modern values*. New York: Vintage.

Howell, Mary C. (1975). *Helping ourselves: Women and the human network*. Boston: Beacon.

Hunnicutt, Benjamin Kline. (1988). *Work without end: Abandoning shorter hours for the right to work*. Philadelphia: Temple University Press.

Hunnicutt, Benjamin Kline. (1993–1994, Winter). The pursuit of happiness: A six-hour day at the Kellogg Company plant liberated time for family and community and provided jobs for the unemployed. *In Context*, pp. 34–38.

Huxley, Aldous. (1953). *Brave new world*. New York: Bantam Books. (Original work published 1932)

Jacobs, Jane. (1961). *The death and life of great American cities*. New York: Vintage.

Jencks, Christopher, et al. (1972). *Inequality: A reassessment of the effect of family and schooling in America*. New York: Basic Books.

Katz, Peter. (1994). *The new urbanism: Toward an architecture of community*. New York: McGraw-Hill.

Keats, John. (1958). *The insolent chariots*. New York: Lippincott.

Keynes, John Maynard. (1932). *Essays in persuasion*. New York: Harcourt, Brace & Co.

Kottak, Conrad Phillip. (1994). *Cultural anthropology* (6th ed.). New York: McGraw-Hill.

Kramer, John L., Pope, Thomas R., and Phillips, Lawrence C. (1996). *Federal taxation: 1997*. Upper Saddle River, NJ: Prentice Hall.

Krantzler, Mel. (1975). *Creative divorce: A new opportunity for personal growth*. New York: Signet Books.

Lasch, Christopher. (1978a). *Haven in a heartless world: The family besieged*. New York: Basic Books.

Lasch, Christopher. (1978b). *The culture of narcissism: American life in an age of diminishing expectations*. New York: Norton.

Lasch, Christopher. (1997). *Women and the common life: Love, marriage, and feminism*, ed. Elizabeth Lasch-Quinn. New York: Norton.

Levitan, Sar A., Belous, Richard S., and Gallo, Frank. (1988). *What's happening to the American family? Tensions, hopes, realities*, rev. ed. Baltimore: Johns Hopkins University Press.

Lewis, Sinclair. (1961). *Babbitt*. New York: Signet Books. (Original work published 1922)

Lubbers, Rudd. (1997, Fall). The Dutch way. *New Perspectives Quarterly, 14* (4), 14–15.

Lynd, Robert S., and Lynd, Helen M. (1929). *Middletown: A study in American culture*. London: Constable & Co.

Malinowski, Bronislaw. (1960). *Argonauts of the western Pacific: An account of native enterprise and adventure in the archipelagoes of Melanesian New Guinea*. New York: Dutton. (Original work published 1922)

Mattox, William R., Jr. (1991, Winter). The parent trap. *Policy Review, 55*, 6–13.

Mayer, Martin. (1958). *Madison Avenue, U.S.A.* New York: Harper & Co.

McLanahan, Sara, and Sandefur, Gary. (1994). *Growing up with a single parent: What hurts, what helps*. Cambridge, MA: Harvard University Press.

Mead, Margaret. (1939). *From the south seas: Studies of adolescence and sex in primitive societies*. New York: William Morrow.

Mead, Margaret. (1949). *Male and female: A study of the sexes in a changing world*. New York: William Morrow.

Mead, Margaret. (1961). *Coming of age in Samoa*. New York: William Morrow. (Original work published 1928)

Mosteller, Frederick. (1995, Summer/Fall). The Tennessee study of class size in the early school grades. *The Future of Children, 5* (2), 113–127.

National Commission on Excellence in Education. (1983). *A nation at risk: The imperative for educational reform*. Washington, DC: U.S. Government Printing Office.

Newman, Oscar. (1972). *Defensible space: Crime prevention through urban design*. New York: Macmillan.

Norquist, John O. (1998). *The wealth of cities: Revitalizing the centers of American life*. Reading, MA: Addison-Wesley.

O'Neill, Nena, and O'Neill, George. (1972). *Open marriage: A new life style for couples*. New York: M. Evans & Company.

Packard, Vance. (1960). *The waste makers*. New York: David McKay.

Parsons, Talcott, Bales, Robert F., et al. (1955). *Family: Socialization and interaction process*. Glencoe, IL: Free Press.

Popenoe, David. (1996). *Life without father: Compelling new evidence that fatherhood and marriage are indispensable for the good of children and society*. Cambridge, MA: Harvard University Press.

Putnam, Robert D. (1995, January). Bowling alone: America's declining social capital. *Journal of Democracy, 6* (1), 65–78.

Putnam, Robert D. (1996, Winter). The strange disappearance of civic America. *The American Prospect*, pp. 34–48.

Renner, Michael. (1988). *Rethinking the role of the automobile* (Worldwatch Paper No. 84). Washington, DC: Worldwatch Institute.

Riesman, David. (1954). *Individualism reconsidered and other essays*. Glencoe, IL: Free Press.

Riesman, David, with Glazer, Nathan, and Denney, Reuel. (1969). *The lonely crowd*. New Haven, CT: Yale University Press. (Original work published 1950).

Schor, Juliet. (1991). *The overworked American: The unexpected decline of leisure*. New York: Basic Books.

Schwartz, Felice. (1990, Winter). Careerus interruptus. *New Perspectives Quarterly, 7* (1), 16–19.

Seeley, John R., Sim, R. Alexander, and Loosley, Elizabeth W. (1956). *Crestwood Heights: A study of the culture of suburban life*. New York: Basic Books.

Siegel, Charles. (1997). *Slow is beautiful: Speed limits as decisions on urban form*. Berkeley, CA: Preservation Institute.

Stacey, Judith. (1991). *Brave new families*. New York: Basic Books.

Stacey, Judith. (1996). *In the name of the family: Rethinking family values in the postmodern age*. Boston: Beacon.

Steinberg, Lawrence. (1996). *Beyond the classroom: Why school reform has failed and what parents need to do*. New York: Simon & Schuster.

Steuerle, C. Eugene. (1999, Spring). Valuing marital commitment: The radical restructuring of our tax and transfer systems. *The Responsive Community, 2* (9), 35–45.

Szasz, Thomas. (1970). *Ideology and insanity: Essays on the psychiatric dehumanization of man*. Garden City, NY: Doubleday Anchor.

Tönnies, Ferdinand. (1963). *Gemeinschaft und Gesellschaft* [Community and society], trans. and ed. Charles P. Loomis. New York: Harper & Row. (Original work published 1887)

U.S. Bureau of Economic Statistics. (1976). *The handbook of basic economic statistics*. Washington, DC: U.S. Government Printing Office.

U.S. Bureau of the Census. (1975). *Historical statistics of the United States, colonial times to 1970*, bicentennial ed. Washington, DC: U.S. Government Printing Office.

U.S. Bureau of the Census. (1996). *Statistical abstract of the United States, 1996*, 116th ed. Washington, DC: U.S. Government Printing Office.

U.S. Department of Commerce and U.S. Bureau of the Census. (1966). *Long-term economic growth: 1860–1965*. Washington, DC: U.S. Government Printing Office.

U.S. Department of Education, National Center for Education Statistics. (1996). *Digest of education statistics 1996*. Washington, DC: U.S. Government Printing Office.

Van Vorst, Mrs. John, and Van Vorst, Marie. (1903). *The woman who toils*. New York: Doubleday, Page & Co.

Wallerstein, Judith, and Blakeslee, Sandra. (1989). *Second chances*. New York: Ticknor & Fields.

Waring, Marilyn. (1988). *If women counted: A new feminist economics*. New York: Harper & Row.

Whitehead, Barbara Dafoe. (1993, April). Dan Quayle was right. *Atlantic Monthly*, pp. 47–84.

Whitehead, Barbara Dafoe. (1997). *The divorce culture*. New York: Knopf.

Whyte, William H. (1956). *The organization man*. New York: Simon & Schuster.

Wilson, William Julius. (1990). *The truly disadvantaged: The inner city, the underclass, and public policy*. Chicago: University of Chicago Press.

Wylie, Phillip. (1942). *A generation of vipers*. New York: Farrar & Rinehart.

INDEX

ABOUT THE AUTHOR

Charles Siegel is the founder of the Preservation Institute. He is the author of *The Preservationist Manifesto* (Northbrae Books, 1996) and of policy studies on economic growth, child care, health insurance reform, mental health care, and other issues. His articles have appeared in *New Perspectives Quarterly, Utne Reader, Whole Earth, Earth Island Journal*, and other magazines. He has also written eight books on computer technology. But he believes his most important qualification for writing this book is that he is a former "househusband": For 5 years, his wife worked while he stayed home to care for his son.